HARVARD HISTORICAL STUDIES

PUBLISHED UNDER THE DIRECTION OF
THE DEPARTMENT OF HISTORY

FROM THE INCOME OF

THE HENRY WARREN TORREY FUND

VOLUME XXXIX

HARVARD HISTORICAL STUDIES

I. The Suppression of the African Slave-Trade to the United States of America, 1638-1870. By W. E. B. DuBois.

II. The Contest over the Ratification of the Federal Constitution in Massachusetts. By S. B. Harding.

III. A Critical Study of Nullification in South Carolina. By D. F. Houston.

IV. Nominations for Elective Office in the United States. By Frederick W. Dallinger.

V. A Bibliography of British Municipal History, including Gilds and Parliamentary Representation. By Charles Gross.

VI. The Liberty and Free Soil Parties in the Northwest. By Theodore Clarke Smith.

VII. The Provincial Governor in the English Colonies of North America. By Evarts Boutell Greene.

VIII. The County Palatine of Durham. A Study in Constitutional History. By G. T. Lapsley.

IX. The Anglican Episcopate and the American Colonies. By A. L. Cross.

X. The Administration of the American Revolutionary Army. By Louis Clinton Hatch.

XI. The Civil Service and the Patronage. By Carl Russell Fish.

XII. The Development of Freedom of the Press in Massachusetts. By C. A. Duniway.

XIII. The Seigniorial System in Canada. By W. B. Munro.

XIV. The Frankpledge System. By William Alfred Morris.

XV. The Public Life of Joseph Dudley. By Everett Kimball.

XVI. Mémoire de Marie Caroline, Reine de Naples. Edited by Robert Matteson Johnston.

XVII. The Barrington-Bernard Correspondence. Edited by E. Channing.

XVIII. The Government of the Ottoman Empire in the Time of Suleiman the Magnificent. By Albert Howe Lybyer.

XIX. The Granger Movement. By S. J. Buck.

XX. Burgage Tenure in Medieval England. By Morley de Wolf Hemmeon.

XXI. An Abridgment of the Indian Affairs transacted in the colony of New York from 1678 to 1751. By Peter Wraxall. Edited with an introduction by Charles Howard McIlwain.

XXII. English Field Systems. By Howard Levi Gray.

XXIII. The Second Partition of Poland. By Robert Howard Lord.

XXIV. Norman Institutions. By Charles Homer Haskins.

XXV. Robert Curthose, Duke of Normandy. By Charles Wendell David.

XXVI. Bismarck's Diplomacy at its Zenith. By Joseph Vincent Fuller.

XXVII. Studies in the History of Medieval Science. By Charles H. Haskins.

XXVIII. The Origins of the War of 1870. New Documents from the German Archives. By Robert H. Lord.

XXIX. The Monroe Doctrine, 1823-1826. By Dexter Perkins.

XXX. The Franco-Russian Alliance, 1890-1894. By W. L. Langer.

XXXI. Fur Trade and Empire. George Simpson's Journal . . . together with accompanying documents. Edited by Frederick Merk.

XXXII. The Schleswig - Holstein Question. By Lawrence D. Steefel.

XXXIII. The Presbyterian Churches and the Federal Union, 1861-1869. By Lewis G. Vander Velde.

XXXIV. The Influence of the Commons on Early Legislation. By Howard L. Gray.

XXXV. The National Workshops. By Donald Cope McKay.

XXXVI. Franz Joseph and Bismarck before 1866. By C. W. Clark.

XXXVII. The Caracas Company 1728-1784. By Roland D. Hussey.

XXXVIII. Great Britain and the Cyprus Convention Policy of 1878. By Dwight E. Lee.

XXXIX. The Fronde. By Paul Rice Doolin.

THE FRONDE

BY

PAUL RICE DOOLIN

*Assistant Professor and Tutor in History and
Literature, Harvard University*

CAMBRIDGE
HARVARD UNIVERSITY PRESS
LONDON: HUMPHREY MILFORD
OXFORD UNIVERSITY PRESS
1935

MGE

"Car pour parler du desordre qui peult aduenir par l'imperfec-
tion des chefz et monarques, il y a plusieurs remedes pour re-
frener leur auctorité absolue, s'ilz sont deprauez et voluntaires.
Et plus encores de ceulx qui pourroient auoir le maniment du
royaume, s'ilz sont du tout imbecilles par faulte d'aage, ou
autrement."

Seyssel in *La Grand' Monarchie de France*

THE author would here express his gratitude to the American Council of Learned Societies and to the Harvard University Committee on Research in the Social Sciences for grants which permitted him to pursue his studies abroad.

CONTENTS

INTRODUCTION xi

CHAPTER

I. RESISTANCE OF THE PARLEMENT (1648–1649) 3
   1. Victory of the Parlement 3
   2. Reform of the Kingdom 10
   3. The Blockade of Paris 21

II. REVOLTS OF THE PRINCES (1649–1653) 29
   1. Arrest of the Princes 29
   2. The First War 36
   3. Condé and the Regent 43
   4. The Second War 50

III. DECLARATIONS OF THE PUBLIC AUTHORITIES . . . 58
   1. Declarations of the Opposition 58
   2. Declarations of the Government 78

IV. DEFENSE OF THE GOVERNMENT 84
   1. Absolutism 84
   2. Theory of Absolutism 100

V. DEFENSE OF THE OPPOSITION (I) 111
   1. The Monarchy limited by Law and the Right of Resistance . 111
   2. Divided Authority under Law. Claude Joly 121

VI. DEFENSE OF THE OPPOSITION (II) 135
   1. Authority of the Parlement, of the Princes, of the Estates . 135
   2. The Minority 148
   3. The Ministériat 152
   4. Theory of Constitutionalism 156

BIBLIOGRAPHY 167
  I. FOR CHAPTERS I AND II 167
  II. FOR CHAPTER III 169
  III. FOR CHAPTER IV 169
  IV. FOR CHAPTERS V AND VI 172

INTRODUCTION

THIS essay is part of a work which I hope sometime to complete, a constitutional history of France in the seventeenth and eighteenth centuries. It has long been my conviction that a term other than "absolute monarchy" should be used to describe the French state of this period.

Many facts point to this conclusion. Even during the personal rule of Louis XIV, when the monarchy reached its height, examples of successful resistance to the King's command are very numerous: Colbert's economic and legal reforms met with strong opposition, and had to be largely abandoned; the long struggle to eliminate Calvinism and Jansenism ended in failure; the two attempts to establish universal direct taxation, the *capitation* and the *dixième*, were unsuccessful. Finally, negotiation with other authorities, the Assembly of the Clergy, the provincial Estates, was one of the chief occupations of the government.

After the death of Louis XIV, successful resistance to the government was more common. To the forces of opposition was added the Parlement of Paris, which had been almost eliminated as a political power by Louis XIV. The Regent restored to the Court a part of the authority which they had formerly exercised; the Parlement laid claim to the rest, and frequently in the course of the reigns of Louis XV and Louis XVI made good their claim.

In fact, then, the power of the King of France in the seventeenth and eighteenth centuries was limited. It might be objected that this does not prove that the state was not legally an absolute monarchy: these examples of successful resistance might be explained by the weakness of the government; the law of the state was the will of the King, but the government lacked the power to enforce the law. On reflection, however, this objection appears to have little weight: that the magistracy and clergy could have been consistently guilty of criminal action is unthinkable.

This hypothesis is confirmed by the explanations of their acts made by the opponents of the government. In every case that I have investigated, opposition is justified by the law. Constitutional precedent is cited, and the citations are good: they can bear the interpretations which are put upon them. It is probable, then, that it might be demonstrated that on many of those frequent occasions when the King's command was successfully opposed, the kingdom of France was a limited monarchy.

This work is a description of the Fronde, the most important act of opposition in this period. I have attempted to show what an examination of the evidence has convinced me is the truth, that this movement rested upon a constitutional theory according to which the will of the King is not law. The question of whether or not this theory was true in fact, of whether the form of the state advocated by the opposition was actually that of France before the reign of Louis XIII, I have not attempted to answer. That the opposition sincerely thought it was, I think there can be no doubt. And this opinion was shared by the government and their supporters: the absolutistic argument, it will be shown, rests not upon the constitution, but upon "reason" and revelation.

The Fronde, it will appear further, was not blindly conservative. To the reason of the absolutists, which was that the end of the state is peace or power, they opposed a rationalization of the constitution, which was that the end of the state is justice, and the Catholic life.

This description of the Fronde differs radically from those of the authorities. Except for Sainte-Aulaire, who found in this movement the principles of the Revolution, none of them has considered it worthy of serious consideration. Lavisse, whose attitude is typical, condemns it as wantonness: "The Fronde," he says, "was in fact a game, but an abominable game." Convinced that it was much more than a game, that great political issues were involved, I have described this event as a political conflict, and not one of personal whims.

Sainte-Aulaire's thesis still persists in the modern judgments of the Fronde, living as best it can with the theory of wantonness. Lavisse, in another passage, glimpses in the Fronde a promise, unfulfilled, of a "beginning of liberty," and quotes the article of the reform of 1648 which guarantees freedom from arbitrary imprisonment, and the one which limits the King's power in taxation. But identification of the Fronde with the Revolution is unhistorical. The rebels of 1648 would have opposed the constitution of 1791 as bitterly as the Parlement under Louis XVI opposed the reforms of Turgot, Necker and Calonne. The concept of revolution is, as we have seen, directly opposed to the professed theory of the movement. The opposition altered the constitution, it is true, but they altered it to make it conform with the ancient constitution of the state; innovation was to them criminal, and the principle of their attacks upon the government.

The essay is divided into two main parts: the first two chapters are a description of the events, the last four an analysis of the explanations of their acts furnished by the parties. Chapter III deals with the official declarations, Chapters IV, V, and VI with the works of apology.

THE FRONDE

CHAPTER I

RESISTANCE OF THE PARLEMENT (1648-1649)

I. VICTORY OF THE PARLEMENT

THE movement which culminated in the first war of the Fronde may be said to have had its beginning in the action of one of the King's attorneys at the *lit de justice* of January 15th, 1648. There the government presented seven fiscal edicts, all but one of which would increase the burden of taxation. The first created twelve new offices of *maître des requêtes*. The second created new offices in the chancelleries. The third was another creation of offices, the possessors of which were to be paid by fees levied on goods entering Paris. The fourth ordered the payment of twenty-five years' dues by the possessors of *francs-fiefs*. By the fifth the tax on the *aisés*, which had met with strong opposition, was abolished. By the sixth one year's revenue was demanded from the holders of property comprised in the royal domain. The seventh was still another creation of offices, in the maréchaussées of France.

The Advocate General, Omer Talon, demanded registration of the edicts, as was customary at a *lit de justice*. But to the dismay of the Regent and the ministers he prefaced his conclusions with a speech in which he indicted the fiscal régime and, what was more important, denied the absolutistic theory of the *lit de justice*, declaring that there was no instance of the use of this means to enforce the King's will upon the Parlement before the year 1563, and that the practice had become common only in the past twenty-five years; by the laws of the kingdom royal edicts were not valid until examined by the Sovereign Courts; to hold that they were verified when the King had caused them

3

to be read and published in his presence was "a kind of illusion in morality and a contradiction in politics."[1]

The opposition of the Advocate General presaged trouble with the judges. It was not long in coming. Two days after the *lit de justice* the Parlement ordered that a complaint of the *maîtres des requêtes* should be entertained against the edict which concerned them, on the ground that the King could not create offices in the Sovereign Courts during his minority. This was the opening move of a struggle between the Regent and the Parlement which lasted for more than three months, until the beginning of May, when it merged with a new controversy over the renewal of the *Paulette*.

On January 18th, the Parlement, all chambers assembled, commenced examination of the edicts registered at the *lit de justice*. This was contrary to tradition, and two days later the Regent ordered Parlement to send her a deputation to explain their action. Molé, First President of the Parlement, the head of the deputation, informed the Queen that the Court had the right to present remonstrances to the King on the subject of edicts registered at a *lit de justice*, citing as authority the edict of February 21, 1641. The Regent consented to the Parlement's continuing examination of the edicts, provided nothing happened "to offend the authority of the King."[2]

It soon became evident that the Parlement would not confine themselves to remonstrances. The first edict examined was the

[1] Talon, *Mémoires*, 209-212.

This speech of Talon's was widely noticed, even abroad: an edition was published in Holland with a Latin commentary. The passage on the *lit de justice* is given in full in Chapter III of this work.

The part of the speech usually mentioned by modern historians is the description of the results of the heavy taxation of the preceding years: "For ten years the country has been ruined, the peasants reduced to sleeping on straw, their furniture sold to pay the taxes; so that to maintain luxury in Paris, millions of innocent persons are forced to live on bread made of bran and oats, hoping for no protection except in their weakness, and owning nothing but their souls, because no means has been devised to sell these at auction."

[2] Talon considered this a great and surprising concession on the part of the government. "It will render useless," he said, "all verifications of edicts which the King may make hereafter, for this right of deliberation will bring with it the right to modify." *Mémoires*, 214.

one which demanded a year's revenue from the holders of the domain. A number of judges were in favor of modifying it. This was not done, but the Court ordered that payment of the tax would not legitimate alienations of the domain made without letters patent. The storm finally broke on February 15th; the Parlement decreed modification of the edict on the *francs-fiefs*. This, it will be remembered, ordered payment of twenty-five years' dues by the possessors. Of these twenty-five years fourteen had elapsed, and the holders were in debt for them to the government. The Parlement limited the edict to these fourteen years.

The government determined to act. The Regent demanded a clear answer to the following question: Did the Parlement pretend "to modify an edict verified the King sitting in his *lit de justice?*" She stated that if the answer was affirmative, since there was no example of a like enterprise against the authority of the King, she would take measures to repress it; if however, the Court intended to proceed by remonstrances, she would be glad to consider them.[3] This move threw the Parlement into confusion. For two weeks they debated the Regent's proposition without arriving at a conclusion. The absolutistic thesis was defended by President de Mesmes; the authority of the Parlement by Broussel, Le Coigneux, Le Cocq de Corbeville. Broussel declared that the right of the Court to sanction royal edicts was an inviolable rule of the constitution. Le Cocq de Corbeville said that if they could not modify edicts registered at a *lit de justice* under a major King, they could do so when the King was a minor.[4] The discussion was finally brought to a close by the government. On March 1st the Queen demanded an immediate answer, and two days later the Parlement yielded. A decree was passed declaring that it was not the intention of the Court to contravene the will of the King and the Queen Regent; to the decree that the edict on the *francs-fiefs* should be executed for

[3] Talon, *Mémoires*, 215.

[4] This information is from a manuscript journal now in the Archives Nationales: *Debats du Parlement de Paris*, etc., No. U. 336. It will be referred to subsequently by the number. These speeches are more fully reported in Chapter III.

the years elapsed only should be added the words *sous le bon plaisir du Roi et de la Reine*; their majesties were to be petitioned to send a declaration to the Court embodying the Parlement's amendment.

The Parlement thus, under threats, confessed to possess no more than the right of remonstrance. But only under threats. The next edict examined, that which created new offices with fees on goods entering Paris, was also modified. The government again insisted and again the Parlement yielded, changing the modification to remonstrances (March 16).

Opposition to the edicts dragged on for a month longer. On April 7th the Parlement presented oral remonstrances against all the edicts; Molé who spoke urged upon the Queen the necessity of relieving the people, who had paid in taxes 300 millions in three years.[5] On April 23rd, the government gave their answer, which was a refusal: public necessity demanded this assistance, and these means were the best that could be devised to obtain the money. The Parlement received this response in silence, to the satisfaction of the ministers, who, Talon says, considered that the storm was past.

The government was over-confident. A week later they took a step which precipitated a much more serious controversy with the Parlement. On April 29th the *droit annuel*[6] was granted to the Sovereign Courts, to the Parlement gratuitously, but to the other three, the Grand Conseil, the Chambre des Comptes, and the Cour des Aides on condition that they renounce their wages for four years. Resistance was immediate and violent. Delegates of the three courts injured by the royal declaration met and voted to solicit the assistance of the Parlement. This was granted, the Parlement on May 13th passing the following resolution, subsequently famous as the Decree of Union: "Considering what has been said as well by the counsellors of the Court as by the deputies of the Grand Conseil, the Chambre des Comptes, and

---

[5] Talon, *Mémoires*, 222.

[6] This was the *Paulette*. Certain offices were hereditary on condition of an annual payment (*droit annuel*) to the crown. The Paulette was renewed periodically; the last term had expired on the first of the year 1648.

the Cour des Aides, on the curtailing of wages and the payment
of the *droit annuel,* union and adjunction of the Parlement with
these three companies is ordered; to which end two counsellors
of each chamber shall be deputed to confer with the deputies of
the aforesaid companies, and on what is done and reported by
them it shall be ordered as is fitting: and meanwhile, following
the decree made in 1615, no one shall be received in the offices
which shall fall vacant except by consent of the widows and
heirs."

The ministers saw danger. According to Talon, some of them
said that the assembly would go so far as to question the legiti-
macy of a foreigner's holding the position of First Minister;
others that they would compel the *Surintendant* to render an
account of his administration. It was proposed to attempt con-
ciliation by substituting a loan for the curtailment of wages, but
this was rejected as weak, and the government on May 18th
answered the Decree of Union by a decree of the Council which
revoked the *droit annuel.*

This move enraged the radical party in the Parlement, centered in the Chambres des Enquêtes. On May 20th the Enquêtes
demanded action on the Decree of Union. Molé, the First President, argued that the revocation of the *droit annuel* had removed
the cause of the decree, and succeeded in postponing the deliberation until May 23rd. When the Court met on that day, the
King's attorneys presented a *lettre de cachet* which forbade assembly of the chambers of the Parlement and the nomination
of deputies. The Advocate General gave as the government's
reason that the proposed union of the Courts was unconstitutional: it was true that meetings of delegates had been held in
the past in the Chambre St. Louis, but these had been to regulate
wages or to provide against public danger; the proposed assembly
came under neither head; "to make of four sovereign companies
a fifth without order from the King and without legitimate authority was a thing without precedent and without reason, a
kind of republic in the monarchy. . . ." The speech ended with
a threat: "The Queen orders me to say to you that she cannot
suffer it since she is obliged to tolerate no diminution of the

King's authority during her regency; she desires that you be warned of her intention, which is that she will employ all means to prevent this deputation and the assembly of those who are deputed, which assembly she considers contrary to the authority of the King, and injurious to her government."[7]

Though the government had forbidden assembly of the chambers of the Parlement, assembly was ordered for May 25th, to consider the *lettre de cachet*. But on the morning of the twenty-fifth the Parlement received an order to send a deputation immediately to the Palais Royal, and in the meantime to refrain from all deliberation.

At the Palace the Parlementary delegation was harshly treated: the Duke of Orleans told them that they had shown themselves consistently opposed to the will of the King and the welfare of the state, and that their conduct was a public scandal; they were informed by the Chancellor that the Regent was determined never to allow the Union, and that it was her will that the Parlement should cease deliberation upon this affair; further assemblies of the chambers of the Parlement were forbidden.

The next day the Parlement was occupied with judicial business, but on the twenty-seventh the Enquêtes broke into the Grand'Chambre, drove out the lawyers who were arguing a case, and forced the First President to call a meeting of the chambers for the next day. They met, and decided to postpone further consideration of the Union until the eighth of June, the Pentecost recess being at hand.

This delay indicated a conciliatory attitude on the part of the Parlement, but on the night after this vote was taken, May 28th, the government took another step which greatly intensified the opposition. The Chambre des Comptes, the Cour des Aides and the Grand Conseil had been forbidden to communicate with one another; this order was disobeyed by the Grand Conseil, which sent two deputies to the Cour des Aides. The two deputies were arrested by order of the Regent and taken to Mézières.

[7] Talon, *Mémoires*, 225.

The next day four more judges were arrested, two of the Grand Conseil and two of the Cour des Aides, the two companies having exchanged deputations on the subject of the first arrests.

The Parlement returned from the Pentecost recess on June 4th determined to act. The Enquêtes invaded the Grand' Chambre and summoned the First President to open debate on "public affairs." Molé refused, on the pretext that assembly had been decided upon for the eighth. The two following days the Enquêtes occupied their places in the Grand'Chambre, but the First President held firm. It was impossible, however, to postpone the deliberation beyond the eighth, and on the seventh the government determined to make one more attempt to secure obedience before resorting to extreme measures. The King's attorneys were instructed again to inform the Parlement that the Queen forbade their discussing the Union. This they did on June 8th; the Advocate General said, as before, that the government held the project unconstitutional; the precedents cited by the Court were rejected as irrelevant. The Parlement refused to obey, and spent the next few days examining their registers in search of authority for their stand. On June 13th the government moved, sending to the Court a decree of the Council quashing the Decree of Union.

The gauntlet was now thrown down, and serious conflict inevitable: having gone so far, neither side could yield without humiliation. The Parlement met the government squarely; on June 15th it was decreed that the Decree of Union should be executed.

This was a bold act, and it infuriated the government. The following day a deputation was summoned to the Palace. There they were told by the Regent that she would know how to distinguish between good servants of the King and the seditious, and that she would punish the latter in such an exemplary manner that posterity would talk of it. A second decree of the Council was read to them which stated that the Decree of May 13th was an act of disobedience full of contempt and injurious to the royal authority, that they had no power but that committed to

them by the King, and that they were guilty of violent usurpation.[8]

The Parlement, embittered by this treatment, the next day,
June 17th, started deliberation on conclusions of the Advocate
General, who proposed remonstrances against the decrees of the
Council. It was immediately apparent that they would go farther
than the conclusions. The ministers lost their nerve.[9] On June
21st, in a conference between the Duke of Orleans and a delegation of the Parlement, they offered satisfaction in the matter of
the *droit annuel*, the release of the imprisoned judges, and even
the assembly in the Chambre St. Louis, provided the deputies
restricted themselves to the "private interests of the four
Companies."[10]

This retreat served only to stiffen the Parlement. After five
days debate, despite the opposition of the First President, it
was determined to extend the deliberations of the Assembly to
public affairs. This conclusion was reported to the Regent on
June 27th, who was told that "nothing would happen in the
conference with the deputies of the other Companies except what
was proper for the King's service."[11]

The government's reply was given to the Parlement on June
30th. It was a complete capitulation: "the Queen found it good
that the Decree of May 13th should be executed, but in consideration of the delicacy of the military situation, she hoped that
the Assembly would meet immediately, and finish within the
week."

2. REFORM OF THE KINGDOM

The Assembly, composed of delegates from the four Sovereign
Courts, met in the Chambre St. Louis on the afternoon of June

[8] Talon, *Mémoires*, 236.

This decree of the Council is an interesting statement of absolutistic theory. It
is discussed in Chapter III.

[9] The quarrel with the Parlement had excited great interest in Paris: according
to the *Histoire du Temps* the judges had been followed to the Palais Royal on June
16th by ten or twelve thousand men. See also d'Ormesson's *Journal*, I, 518-519.

[10] U. 336, 184-185.

[11] U. 336, 192-203.

30th, a few hours after the Parlement had been informed of the consent of the Regent.[12] They remained in session until the end of July, and between June 30th and July 12th drew up twenty-seven articles, which aimed at a radical reformation of the institutions of the monarchy.[13] The Assembly had no authority to legislate; their conclusions were recommendations, which were reported to the Parlement, where they were debated and acted upon.

On July 4th, the Parlement took action on two of the articles agreed upon in the first meeting of the Assembly of the Chambre St. Louis. A decree was passed which revoked the intendants and "all extraordinary commissions not verified," and also ordered the Procureur Général to inform against the "bad administration of the finances."[14]

This act of the Parlement was an assumption of legislative authority, and a move which touched the government in a vital spot. The ministers in haste called upon the Duke of Orleans to use his influence to bring the Parlement to moderation. He occupied his seat in the Court on July 6th. The Advocate General reported as follows the argument of the government against the decree: although the Regent recognized that the proposed remedies were legitimate, that "the commissions of intendants of justice and all others not verified in the Sovereign Courts were forbidden by certain ordinances," she considered the reform at this time, when the armies were engaged on all frontiers, very impolitic; investigation of the financial administration would persuade the people that they were discharged of their debts to the government.[15] The Duke of Orleans proposed a

[12] The delegates had met on June 16th, but had done nothing. *Journal du Parlement*, June 16. They numbered 31: 11 from the Parlement, 2 *maîtres des requêtes*, 6 from the Grand Conseil, 6 from the Chambre des Comptes, 6 from the Cour des Aides.

[13] The text of the 27 Articles is given in Isambert, XVII, 72-84.

[14] There was an interesting debate on whether the Court should proceed by remonstrance or by decree. It is reported in Chapter III.

[15] Talon, *Mémoires*, 245-246.

This speech of the Advocate General is very interesting. He says (p. 246) that the institution of the intendants is fifteen years old: "It is not since the regency that the intendants have been sent into the provinces; for fifteen years they have

conference between himself and a delegation of the Parlement on the subject of the decree, and urged that in the meantime execution be suspended. The Court argued for two days on the suspension of the decree; finally, on July 7th, the conference was accepted, and *tacito senatusconsulto* execution of the decree suspended for the duration of the conference.[16]

On July 8th delegates of the four Sovereign Courts (the Parlement had insisted that the other courts be represented at the conference) met the Duke of Orleans, Mazarin, and the Chancellor in the Luxembourg. It was a stormy session. The Chancellor and the Minister urged the same reasons that the Advocate General had set forth on July 6th. The delegates refused to listen; President Novion of the Parlement said that the intendants were themselves *partisans*, and interested in the affairs of which they were judges; that it would be justice to repudiate the King's debts, since the financiers had profited enormously in the past years. At last Mazarin, "*pressé, excité, importuné,*" consented to a royal declaration abolishing the intendants.[17] Consideration of the clause in the decree relating to the financial administration was postponed to the next meeting of the conference.[18] The government, though forced to yield on the intendants, had obtained that the reform be ordered by the King.

Three days later, the eleventh, a royal declaration was sent to the Parlement which revoked the commissions of all the intendants except those in the frontier provinces. This produced an uproar in the Court, the judges crying that they had been betrayed, that this was contrary to the agreement reached in the conference. The Duke of Orleans assured them that the intendants retained would have no power in justice or finance, would be only assistants to the Governors, but failed to satisfy

been established on occasion (*selon les occasions*), and for eleven whole years there have been intendants in all the provinces."

Three thousand financial officers had been deprived of their functions by the intendants, and also of their wages, which totaled 9,000,000 a year. Talon, 245.

[16] The *Histoire du Temps* says (p. 114) that suspension was voted for three days.

[17] Talon, *Mémoires*, 247.

[18] Several more conferences were held in the next few days.

them. The government withdrew the declaration and returned it on July 16th modified to include the Duke of Orleans' explanation. The King declared that the institution of the intendants was contrary to the "ancient forms," and that they were revoked except in the provinces of Languedoc, Burgundy, Provence, Lyonnais, Picardy and Champagne, "in which provinces, the intendants which shall be by us commissioned shall not be empowered to interfere in the imposition and raising of our moneys, nor perform any function in the administration of justice (*de juridiction contentieuse*), but shall be entitled to be near the Governors in the said provinces, to assist them in the execution of their powers. . . ."[19] The Parlement registered this declaration with the amendment that the intendants retained should bring their commissions to the Court to be registered.

On July 13th a second declaration had been brought to the Parlement, on the subject of the investigation of the finances. The government had countered the decree of the Parlement by ordering the establishment of a *Chambre de Justice*. This too was found unsatisfactory and rejected. It was returned modified on July 16th, with the edict on the intendants. The Parlement accepted it, but voted that remonstrances should be presented to the Regent to the effect that the *Chambre de Justice* should be composed of members of the Sovereign Courts, and nominated by the Courts.

Meanwhile the Parlement was engaged in even more important business, discussion of articles of the Chambre St. Louis which broached the fundamental issue of authority in taxation: by Article 2, the Assembly had proposed that the taille be reduced by one-fourth, and all arrears up to and including the year 1646 remitted; by Article 6 "no impositions or taxes should be made except by virtue of edicts and declarations well and duly verified in the Sovereign Courts, to whom cognizance of these matters belongs, with liberty of suffrage." On July 14th the government, in the hope of forestalling the Parlement, presented a royal declaration which stated that *in the future* no taxes should be imposed except by edicts or declarations well and duly verified. The

[19] Talon, *Mémoires*, 251.

Parlement registered the declaration with an amendment which altered it radically. This reads: "The Court has ordered and declared that henceforth there shall be no impositions or taxes in the Kingdom except by virtue of Edicts verified in the Court. All those have been revoked and are revoked which have been made by virtue of Declarations published by the Chancellor (*publiées au sceau*) and Decrees of the Council, and it is forbidden to continue them on penalty of death. And as regards the Declarations verified in the Cour des Aides and Chambre des Comptes, the Court orders that they shall have effect only for the present year, and for the year 1649, if the war lasts so long, and without thereby establishing precedent (*sans tirer à conséquence*). The publication of the Declaration shall be suspended until a schedule has been drawn up of the goods and merchandise, and of what they should pay by virtue of the present decree."[20]

As regards reduction of the taille, Parlement endorsed the recommendation of one-fourth made by the Assembly of the Chambre St. Louis. The government offered to meet them half way; in a declaration of July 18th all arrears up to the year 1647 were remitted, and the taille reduced by one-eighth for the years 1648 and 1649. The Parlement registered the declaration, but ordered that the Regent be petitioned to increase the reduction to one-fourth, and further, that the declaration, with the resolution of the Court, should be published.

The next moves of the Parlement the government found even more disturbing. Between the twenty-first and the twenty-fourth the subject of the government's debts was discussed. A recommendation of the Chambre St. Louis, that the farm of the taille be abolished, was accepted. It was then proposed that the government's obligations to the tax farmers should be repudiated, and even that the financiers be prosecuted. If these propositions were put into effect the state's credit would be ruined. The ministers decided to resort to a *lit de justice*.

The government was favored by a short recess of the Parle-

---

[20] This quotation is from the *Histoire du Temps*, 129. See also Talon, *Mémoires*, 249, and the *Journal du Parlement*, at this date.

ment (July 25-29) and by news of a victory, the taking by assault of the city of Tortose by Marshal Schomberg. On the twenty-ninth a thanksgiving service, attended by the whole court in great pomp, was held at Notre Dame, and on the thirty-first the King came to the Parlement.

The edict which the government ordered registered was carefully drawn.[21] The King confessed that many abuses had crept into the government in the past years, but protested that by the constitution reform must be initiated by royal authority; the assembly in the Chambre St. Louis was to cease immediately. When circumstances permitted he would summon a council and by their advice reëstablish order. For the present, the following reforms were feasible and ordered: encroachments of the Royal Council upon the jurisdictions of the other courts were to cease; beginning in 1649 the taille was reduced by one-fourth, the charges upon the taille first deducted; in the future no new taxes were to be imposed except by edicts "well and duly verified," but the taxes then in force should be continued until circumstances permitted reduction; a schedule of the tariff dues of the city of Paris was to be drawn up by the Council; wages of the officers were in part restored; abuses in the administration of the *rentes* of Paris were to be remedied; the edict of 1645 on the domain, and the decree of the Council on the *toisé des maisons* were revoked; the offices of *maître des requêtes* established at the *lit de justice* of January 15th, 1648 were abolished.[22] After the reading of the declaration the Chancellor announced that the King accorded the continuation of the *droit annuel* to the Sovereign Companies, without condition.

The King's declaration contradicted certain of the Parlementary decrees of the past weeks, and ignored many of the recommendations of the Chambre St. Louis. Controversy began immediately on these points and lasted nearly three months, eventuating in the defeat of the government.

On August 5th, five days after the *lit de justice*, the Parlement

---

[21] The edict is given in full by Talon, *Mémoires*, 256-259. It will be discussed in Chapter III.

[22] I have omitted several articles which seem of minor importance.

appointed a commission to examine the royal declaration, and the remaining articles of the Chambre St. Louis; however, out of deference to the wishes of the Duke of Orleans, whose intervention had again been obtained by the ministers, further consideration of these matters in court was postponed to August 17th. The commission reported on that day, and the Parlement immediately set to work, starting with the first article of the royal declaration, on which they decreed remonstrances. On the nineteenth they went farther, ordering that instead of the article in the royal declaration which provided for the establishment of the Paris tariff by the Council, a decree of the Parlement of July 20th should be executed, which read that the tariff should be drawn up by a commission of the Court. This, as Talon says, "was to order that the decree of the Parlement should be executed and that the declaration of the King should not."[23] Two days later the Court decreed that the financiers who had advanced money to the King on the reduction of the salaries of the officers should be prosecuted.

On the following day, August 22nd, news arrived of the Prince of Condé's great victory at Lens, and the government determined to use force. Immediately after the Te Deum at Notre Dame, August 26th, two of the counsellors of the Parlement, Broussel and Blancmesnil, were arrested, and others ordered into exile.

The government's blow miscarried miserably. The whole city sprang to arms in defense of the Parlement, and on the next day the Regent was forced to consent to the release of the prisoners and the return of the exiles.[24] The Court made a slight concession, agreeing to confine themselves until September 7th, the day of the opening of the long recess, to the *rentes* on the Hôtel de Ville, the drawing up of the tariff, and the execution of the

---

[23] Talon, *Mémoires*, 262.

This produced another discussion on the authority of the Court in regard to edicts registered at a *lit de justice*. It is reported in the *Journal du Parlement*, and will be discussed in Chapter III.

[24] August 26-28 are the famous Days of the Barricades. A description with new details has been recently published: *La Fronde à Paris*, by H. Courteault.

decrees already made.[25] On the twenty-ninth a commission was appointed to inform against the financiers named in the decree of August 21st.

The government's failure ruined their authority. The Queen and Mazarin were contemptuously insulted in anonymous pamphlets; in Paris and the vicinity revenue from taxation fell to practically nothing. On September 6th the Regent was forced to consent to the continuation of the Parlement into the recess.

The ministers decided again to try intimidation. On the 13th of September, with elaborate precautions, the court quit the capital and took up residence at Rueil. On the eighteenth the Count of Chavigny was arrested, and the Marquis de Châteauneuf exiled to Berri. These two persons, former ministers, were known to have relations with some of the radical leaders in the Parlement. The next step in the government's program was to order the Parlement out of Paris; in case of resistance they would bring up troops from the frontier.[26]

But the Parlement was on its guard. On September 22nd, on the proposition of Viole, President of one of the chambers of Enquêtes, it was decreed that the Regent should be petitioned to bring the King back to Paris, and that the Duke of Orleans, the Prince of Condé, and the Prince of Conti should be requested to take their places in Parlement "to deliberate upon affairs necessary to the security and welfare of the state." In the debate Mazarin was mentioned by name, and reference made to the decree of 1617, which had closed the King's Council to foreigners. The next day a decree of the Council quashed that of the Parlement. The Court replied by ordering that remonstrances should be made in writing, that the deliberation should be continued, and that measures should be taken for the defense of the city.

---

[25] Lavisse, *France*, VII, Part I, 39 says that the Queen agreed to release the prisoners on condition that the Parlement promise to confine themselves to the administration of justice, and that the Court *prit à peu près l'engagement qui lui était demandé*. This is an important error: the subsequent acts of the Parlement and the government can be understood only as results of a victory of the Court. The text of the Parlement's decree is given in U. 336, pp. 397-398.

[26] This has been established by Chéruel from Mazarin's *carnets*. Chéruel, *Minorité de Louis XIV*, III, 71-77.

War now seemed imminent. But on September 24th the government suddenly reversed its policy and proposed negociations between the Parlement and the Lieutenant General and the Princes.[27] The Parlement accepted, and on the twenty-fifth the first conference was held in the Duke of Orleans' residence at Rueil. Through him, the government offered to terminate all matters in dispute with the Parlement: the Paris tariff, the King's declaration of July 31st, and the remaining articles of the Chambre St. Louis.

In the course of the next ten days five conferences were held on these subjects, in which rapid progress was made, the government yielding on almost all points. The Parlement met serious resistance only in the amount of the reduction of the taille, the Paris tariff, and the famous article "on public security" of the Chambre St. Louis.

On this last subject the debates were long and very interesting. The recommendation of the Chambre St. Louis had read: "No subjects of the King, of whatever quality and condition they may be, shall be held prisoner longer than twenty-four hours without being interrogated, according to the ordinances, and given over to their natural judges, and the jailors, captains, and all others who shall hold them, shall be held responsible for infractions of the law in their own and private names." In the conference of October 1st the Chancellor said that the Regent could not possibly accord this article; it was a right "which had been exercised in all ages and was absolutely necessary in all states, that of arresting those who by cabals, intrigues, plots and other like manner may trouble the tranquility of states, which crimes ought not to be revealed or known in public; that there was a great difference between public and private justice, between the government of the state and the distribution of justice to individuals. This last had been provided for by the ordinances, which required that judges who held prisoners were obliged to

---

[27] The reason for this change of policy is a matter of dispute: Bazin, *France*, I, 351-352, thinks Mazarin was intimidated by the threat to reënact the decree of 1617; Chéruel, *Minorité de Louis XIV*, III, 85-87, that the government had come to fear that they would not be supported by Condé.

interrogate them, and to try them . . . but in public justice, in the conduct and administration of the state, in which one cannot err twice, it should be in the discretion of sovereigns to arrest those upon whom suspicion falls, about whom there is fear that they may abuse the positions in which they find themselves; that on these occasions formalities are useless, because in affairs of this quality the event is of too great consequence, and just as in private crimes (*crimes particuliers*) it is more expedient that a hundred guilty escape than that a single innocent person perish, in the government of states it is more expedient that a hundred innocent persons suffer than that the state perish by the fault of an individual."[28] To this the First President of the Parlement replied that there was great difference between rare and singular circumstances which could not be legislated on, and common and ordinary things for which the law was desired.[29] Under pressure the government finally compromised, offering the royal officers immunity, but reserving the right to imprison other subjects of the King for a period of six months. This compromise, we shall see, was accepted, with alterations, by the Parlement.

The conferences were brought to a close on October 4th and the Parlement was empowered to draw up a declaration embodying the results. For the next two weeks the Court occupied itself with this task, and with negotiations with the government over certain tax reductions which had not been settled in the conferences. The declaration was completed on October 22nd, presented to the Regent, and the same day sealed by the Chancellor. On October 24th it was published in the Parlement and registered.

[28] Talon, *Mémoires*, 282.

[29] According to the *Journal du Parlement*, Molé said that before the reign of Louis XIII arbitrary imprisonment had been very rare: "If there had been some examples, it was so rare, and the evil passed so quickly, that the remedy was as prompt as the evil. In the time of King Henry the Great, in 1597, there had been an example, but it lasted only two days and the order to retire to his house had been immediately revoked. In 1561 there was another example, but now this disorder had passed into Custom, and so it was necessary to find assurance against it, and to give it by the law, by words, and by the release of M. de Chavigny."

The Regent in this act accorded almost the complete program
of reform of the Assembly of the Chambre St. Louis. By the
first article, the taille for the year 1648 was reduced by a fifth.
The second article decreased considerably the indirect taxes, the
Paris tariff, the *aides*, the *cinq grosses fermes*, the *gabelle*. The
third provided guaranties against abuses in the award of tax
farms. By the fourth, the wages of the royal officers were in part
restored; it was forbidden to touch them for four years, and after
that time only by virtue of edicts and declarations well and duly
verified. Articles 5 and 6 remedied abuses in the administration
of the *rentes*. Article 7 ordered the possessors of the royal domain
to bring their titles to the Parlement and the Chambre des Comptes for verification. By article 8 the use of *comptants* was limited
to the "secret and important affairs of the state." Article 9
stated that no new offices of judicature or finance should be
created in the next four years, and after that only by virtue of
edicts well and duly verified. Article 10 provided against the tax
farmers' placing their property out of reach of the King's mort-
gages, and those of their creditors. Article 11 ordered the suppression of a number of recently created offices in Paris. Article
12 abolished all trading privileges within the kingdom and prohibited the importation of certain foreign products. Article 13
provided against disorders of the King's soldiers. Article 14
elaborately protected the jurisdictions of the courts against encroachments by the King through the agency of the Council
and special commissions. Article 15 and last dealt with the
matter of "public security." It reads as follows: "We desire also
that none of our subjects of whatever quality and condition, be
treated criminally in the future except in accordance with the
forms prescribed by the laws of our Kingdom, and the ordinances,
and not by commissions and chosen judges, and that the ordinance of King Louis XI, of the eleventh of the month of October
1467, be kept and observed according to its form and tenor; in
interpretation and execution of which none of our officers of our
Sovereign Courts or others shall be troubled or disturbed in the
exercise and practice of their charges by *lettres de cachet*, or other-

wise, in any way or manner, the whole in conformity with the said ordinance, and their privileges."[30]

This was a great victory. The *Histoire du Temps*, which ends at this point, concludes with the following sentences: "You (the Parlement) are now masters of the battlefield; you will know how to make good use of the victory won, and the honor of the triumph. Such are the wishes of all good Frenchmen, and of all who love the public weal and the service of the Prince."[31]

3. THE BLOCKADE OF PARIS

The declaration of October 22nd, in the opinion of the Prime Minister, "abolished the best part of the royalty." The government immediately laid their plans to bring the Parlement to terms by besieging the capital; the Declaration would then be withdrawn on the ground that it had been accorded under compulsion.[32]

This project was sensed by the judges, who kept a sharp eye on the ministers, and met every move. After preliminary skirmishing issue was joined on the ninth of December, when the Enquêtes demanded assembly of the chambers of the Parlement to deliberate upon infractions of the Declaration, and suspicious movements of troops in the vicinity of Paris. The First President succeeded in postponing the assembly for several days, but on December 16th, the chambers met, the Lieutenant General, the Prince of Condé, and several Dukes and Peers in their places.

The government was defended by the Duke of Orleans. The most serious of the charges of the Court was that the military authorities had been taking tailles for the support of the armies in excess of the amount ordered in the Declaration. The Duke insisted that these were "simple advances," which would not increase the total payments. It was a disorderly session. President Viole, who urged in veiled terms action against the Minister, was interrupted by the Lieutenant General.

[30] Talon, *Mémoires*, 293-297.
[31] *Histoire du Temps*, 240.
[32] Chéruel, *Minorité de Louis XIV*, III, 91-94.

The following day the debate was continued, and a commission appointed to investigate breaches of the Declaration. On the nineteenth, after another stormy session, a decree was passed forbidding all levies of money by the military authorities; further, the Procureur Général was rudely pressed to render an account of the prosecution of the financiers, ordered by the Parlement.

A few days later there was another dispute. The Cour des Aides had made important amendments to the Declaration of October 22nd, among which was an article forbidding farming the tailles, and loaning money on the tailles, on penalty of death, and the Chambre des Comptes had modified the article which restricted the *comptants* to secret and important affairs of state by limiting the *comptants* to 3,000,000 a year.[33] The government sent a declaration to the Chambre des Comptes which violated these amendments, and which the Chambre des Comptes refused to register. On December 30th the Parlement intervened and demanded communication of the royal declaration. The Chambre des Comptes showed themselves inclined to resist the Parlement in defense of their jurisdiction, but on January 2nd the government withdrew the declaration.

This concession produced a lull in the hostilities and facilitated the execution of the project which the government had been meditating for the past four months, and for which they were now ready. The fifth of January was a holiday, the Fête des Rois. Shortly after midnight, the royal family and the principal ministers slipped out of Paris and went to St. Germain. The next day the city government of Paris was informed that the King had been obliged to depart in order not to remain exposed to the pernicious designs of certain officers of the Parlement who had relations with the declared enemies of the state, had several times attacked his authority, and had gone so far as to conspire to seize his person.

---

[33] The modifications of the Declaration ordered by the financial courts were very extensive. Besides the two mentioned in the text, one other deserves notice: on Article I the Chambre des Comptes ordered that the reduction of the taille should be for the "present year and *those following*." The texts of the decrees of the two courts are given by Talon, *Mémoires*, 307-311, and 313-314.

The Parlement, informed of the government's action, immediately decreed that measures be taken for the police of the city, and to prevent supplies from being cut off. On January 7th a messenger arrived from St. Germain with letters patent transferring the Parlement to Montargis.[34] The Court, informed of the content of the letters by the Advocate General, refused to open them on the ground that they should have been addressed to the King's attorneys rather than to the Parlement. They then ordered that the King's attorneys should go to the Regent to demand the names of the persons referred to in the King's letter to the Hôtel de Ville, and to beg her to withdraw the troops which had been concentrated in the neighborhood of the capital.

At St. Germain the Parlement's envoys were harshly treated. After having been made to wait for hours in the cold, they were informed by the Chancellor that the Regent was determined to make the Parlement obey at any price, that Paris would be besieged unless the Court obeyed the order of translation. The Advocate General delivered the narration of the mission on the eighth, and the same day the Parlement decreed that Mazarin, author of all the disorders of the state, and of the present evil, enemy of the King and his state, should quit the court and the kingdom, on penalty of outlawry.

War was now inevitable, and on the ninth the Parlement started to organize the defense of the city. The Court was supported by the Chambre des Comptes, the Cour des Aides, and the city government, and made rapid progress. Before the end of the month several regiments were raised and equipped, officered by nobles who, under the leadership of three princes of royal blood, the Prince of Conti, the Duke of Longueville, and the Duke of Beaufort, had come in large numbers to offer their swords to the Parlement. Supreme command was given to the Prince of Conti.

Measures were also taken to obtain aid from outside: letters were written to the other parlements explaining the conflict and

---

[34] The Parlement was suppressed by a royal declaration dated January 23rd. This is an important statement of absolutistic doctrine; it will be discussed in Chapter III.

urging their support.[35] Two of them, Aix and Rouen, having quarrels of long standing with the government over the establishment of "semesters,"[36] voted to make common cause with the Parlement of Paris. At Aix open war broke out between the Parlement and the Governor, the Count of Alais. Rouen on January 20th opened its gates to the Duke of Longueville, Governor of Normandy, who had been deprived of his office by the Regent. The Duke immediately set about raising troops for the relief of Paris. The government, with the intention, doubtless, of weakening the Parlement on January 23rd issued letters ordering elections for the Estates General, which would meet at Orleans on March 15th.

From the military standpoint the blockade of Paris was a trivial affair. Condé, who commanded the government forces, had only seven or eight thousand men and was obliged to confine himself to the occupation of positions which dominated the important roads and waterways. Fighting was limited largely to skirmishes between the royal troops and the escorts of provision trains. On February 8th occurred the only important engagement of the war, the capture of Charenton by Condé.

This was a considerable success, but by this time the government had had enough. They had hoped that a show of force would bring the city and the Parlement quickly to terms; they had been mistaken, and were now confronted with revolts in the provinces.[37] Even more serious were reports that Turenne, who commanded the King's army in Germany, was attempting to persuade his officers to march to the assistance of Paris. Accordingly, on February 17th, when the King's attorneys presented themselves at St. Germain to explain the Parlement's refusal to receive a royal herald, and to express the submission and obedience of the Court, they were not too coldly received.

[35] The remonstrances of January 21st were an elaborate defense of the Parlement, Talon, *Mémoires*, 323-328. They will be discussed in Chapter III.

[36] The number of judges was doubled, the old court and the new appointees serving in turn.

[37] For the revolts in the provinces see Chéruel, *Minorité de Louis XIV*, III, Chapter V.

The government's inclination was doubtless strengthened by an event which occurred two days later: on the motion of the Prince of Conti the Parlement received an ambassador from the Archduke Leopold, Governor of the Spanish Netherlands, who presented a letter supposedly written by his master, which accused Mazarin of offering peace to Spain at any price, so that he would be free to deal with the rebellion; the Archduke, considering this proposal dishonorable, and that Mazarin had no authority since he had been condemned by the Parlement, offered to treat of peace with the Parlement.[38] The Court voted to send a deputation to the Regent to inform her of this embassy, and to beg her to withdraw the troops.

The deputation of the Parlement was received at St. Germain on the twenty-fifth. They were given a letter which attacked the Court bitterly for having usurped the King's authority in receiving an embassy from a foreign power with which he was at war, but were informed that the government would confer with the Parlement, and that during the conference supplies would be allowed to enter the city.

On March 1st the Parlement accepted the conference, which opened on the fourth at Rueil. The delegation from Paris numbered twenty-two, twelve from the Parlement, three from the city government, one maître des requêtes, three from the Chambre des Comptes, three from the Cour des Aides. The government was represented by the Lieutenant General, the Prince of Condé, and a number of the ministers, including Mazarin. The delegation refused to treat with the Cardinal, and it was arranged that the two parties should meet separately, exchanging their proposals by deputies.

The government began by taking a very high tone: the Parlement should quit Paris and go to St. Germain until further orders; twenty-five persons of the various official bodies were to be exiled; the city government should demand pardon from the King; the amendments made by the Chambre des Comptes and the Cour des Aides to the Declaration of October 22nd should be revoked; no assembly of the chambers of Parlement should

[38] Talon, *Mémoires*, 336.

be held for three years, and then assembly could be called only by vote of the Grand'Chambre and only persons of twenty years service should be allowed to attend.[39] All this, though, was for the purpose of bargaining; in the treaty signed on March 12th little remained of the government's original demands.

The Treaty of Rueil contained twenty-one articles, of which the following were the most important. Article 2 stated that the Parlement should go to St. Germain, where the King would hold a *lit de justice* at which a declaration embodying the articles accorded would be published; the Parlement could then return to Paris. By Article 3, no assembly of the chambers of Parlement was to be held in the year 1649. Article 4 reads: "In the *narré* of the declaration which is to be published, it will be stated that it is the will of His Majesty that the Declarations of May, July and October, 1648, verified in the Parlement, shall be executed, except as concerns borrowing, as will be explained hereafter." The article referred to here is 12, which allows the King to borrow whatever sums he deems necessary for the present year and the following, paying interest *au denier douze*. Articles 17 and 18 gave satisfaction to the allies of the Parlement, promising suppression of the "semesters" in the Parlements of Aix and Rouen. Article 20 gave the Parlement a share in the negotiations with Spain. It reads: "When His Majesty sends deputies to treat of peace with Spain, he will willingly choose some one of the officers of the Parlement of Paris to assist in the said treaty, with the same power as that given the others."[40] Among the signatures to the treaty was that of Mazarin.

On March 13th the Parlement assembled to consider the treaty. It was a tumultuous session. The news that Mazarin had signed had spread through the city, and the Palace of Justice was invaded by a mob numbering a thousand persons, who demanded the expulsion of the Minister. This disorder was promoted by the Generals, who saw personal advantages in a continuation of the war. The Court decreed that the treaty

[39] Bazin, *France*, I, 449-450.
[40] The text of the treaty of Rueil is given in Isambert, XVII, 161-163.

should not be read, and that the deputies should return to St. Germain to treat for the Generals.

This decision was reversed two days later. On the fourteenth a letter from the government was delivered to the Parlement demanding immediate registration of the treaty; the reason for the Parlement's delay, the King said, was that they were expecting news from the Marquis of Noirmoutier, who had been sent to the Archduke Leopold to procure his entrance into the kingdom. The letter ended, however, with the statement that the Regent would listen, after the registration, to a deputation of the Parlement in regard to the interests of the Generals and any matters which might be objected to in the treaty. On March 15th, with the Palace of Justice closely guarded, the Parlement decreed acceptance of the treaty, and that the Regent should be petitioned to revoke three articles: the *lit de justice* at St. Germain, the prohibition of assemblies of the Parlement for the year 1649, and the reëstablishment of loans; the deputation which would treat of these matters would also negotiate for the Generals.[41]

The new conference opened on March 16th at St. Germain between the deputies of the Parlement (the other companies were not represented) and a number of the ministers, without Mazarin. The Generals had their own deputation, headed by the Duke of Brissac.

The discussion lasted for three weeks. Throughout this time the Generals did their utmost to bring about rupture of the negociations. On March 22nd the Parlement was informed in the name of the Prince of Conti that the Archduke had crossed the frontier, and that he had come in the service of the Parlement, and to negotiate peace between the two crowns. On the 23rd the Generals' remaining deputy quit the conference. The majority of the Parlement, however, and the delegation favored peace, and agreement was reached in the conference on March 29th.

Under the pressure of the Spanish invasion the government

41 Talon, *Mémoires*, 347.

had yielded on all points in dispute with the Parlement.[42] The
articles dealing with the *lit de justice* and the assemblies of the
Parlement were suppressed, and satisfaction was given in the
matter of loans. The Treaty of Rueil had ordered the surrender
of the Bastille to the government; this clause was omitted, and
the fortress remained in the hands of the Parlement. To the
Generals great concessions were made in the form of grants of
money, offices, etc.[43]

The amended treaty was submitted to the Parlement on March
31st. The Generals protested violently, but were able to delay
acceptance of the declaration which embodied the settlement only
a day. It was registered on April 1st, the Parlement voting that
a deputation be appointed to thank the King and Queen for
giving peace to their people, to petition them to return to Paris,
and to beg them to consider further the interests of the Generals.
The troops were ordered discharged.

On April 5th a thanksgiving service was celebrated at Notre
Dame, and on the 14th an assembly of the chambers of the
Parlement met to hear the report of the deputation which had
been sent to St. Germain.[44]

[42] For the importance of the Spanish invasion in determining the policy of the
government see the *Lettres du Cardinal Mazarin*, III, 318.

[43] Talon, *Mémoires*, 353.

[44] It seems obvious that the blockade of Paris ended in the defeat of the government. This is the opinion, too, of Talon, who says, *Mémoires*, 356, that the government were obliged to "relâcher tout ce qu'ils ont voulu." Chéruel at this point
fails to conclude, and in the next volume, *Minorité de Louis XIV*, IV, 226 says
that this war ended in a victory for Mazarin: "Il se rappelait qu'en 1649 il avait
triomphé de la Fronde parlementaire par l'épée de Condé."

CHAPTER II

REVOLTS OF THE PRINCES (1649-1653)

1. ARREST OF THE PRINCES

FOR several months after peace was signed, the Regent kept away from Paris, where quiet had by no means been restored. Anonymous pamphleteers continued their attacks upon the government. In June occurred a clash between the two parties, which seems trivial, but which indicates the state of feeling. A number of young lords of the party of the government, led by the Count of Jarzé, came to Paris and showed themselves in the Tuileries gardens, where the Duke of Beaufort and his suite were strolling. They then boasted that they had defied the enemy in his stronghold. Beaufort determined to have revenge. On the 18th of June Jarzé and his followers again came to the Tuileries, to dine at Renard's, a fashionable restaurant at the west end of the gardens. The Duke entered the restaurant with a numerous following, asked Jarzé if he had violins, for he was going to make him and his friends dance, and then picked up one end of the table cloth, dumping the dishes on the banqueters. The government considered prosecuting Beaufort, but were dissuaded by the Attorney General, who asserted that this action would cause an uprising in Paris, where Beaufort had an enormous popular following.[1]

The pamphleteers, who became more and more violent, caused the government deep concern. On July 3rd the Duke of Orleans called a special assembly of the city authorities and urged that action be taken against them. Shortly afterward a printer named

---

[1] Talon, *Mémoires*, 360.
Beaufort's bravery in the War of Paris had made him the idol of the mob. His enemies called him *le Roi des Halles*.

Morlot was caught in the act of printing verses which charged the Queen with improper conduct. He was condemned to death by the Parlement, but was delivered by a mob on his way to the gibbet.

Despite these evidences of hostility, the government by the middle of August felt it safe to return to Paris. On August 18th the King, the Regent, and the ministers entered the capital, and were received with acclamations. On September 5th the King's birthday was celebrated with the customary enthusiasm.

But if the government could feel fairly sure of Paris, they were confronted with grave difficulties in other quarters. Serious disorders had broken out in the provinces, all of which, Talon says, were working for their liberation.[2] In Provence war between the Count of Alais and the Parlement had started anew. The Estates of Languedoc had asserted their right to consent to taxation, of which they had been deprived by Richelieu, and those of Dauphiné had done the same.

In Guyenne there had been serious fighting since the close of the war of Paris. Hostility had long existed between the Governor of the province, the Duke d'Épernon, and the Parlement of Bordeaux, which was supported by the city. The quarrel came to a head in the spring of 1649, and the government dispatched one of their diplomats, d'Argenson, to negotiate an accord.

The current dispute was the resistance of the Parlement and the city to the Governor's attempt to introduce supplies into the Chateau Trompette, which dominated the city, and to the construction of a fort at Libourne, which would give the Governor control of the Dordogne. D'Argenson secured agreement to a compromise: the city would allow the Governor to introduce 200 sacks of flour into the castle, and the Governor would abandon the fort at Libourne. The city carried out their part of the bargain, but the Governor continued work on the fort. At this an army composed of peasants and workmen, officered by counsellors of the Parlement, sallied forth from Bordeaux to take and destroy the fort. They were met by d'Épernon at the head of

---

[2] Talon, *Mémoires*, 361.

a force of trained soldiers, and cut to pieces (May 16). D'Épernon entered Bordeaux, but was unable to reëstablish his authority. He then obtained from the government interdiction of the Parlement, but when he attempted to enforce it, the populace rose, and drove him from the city.

These last events occurred in the months of June, July, and August.[3] Before the end of the summer the Parlement of Paris showed themselves inclined to intervene. In the middle of July they had received an informal communication from Provence which they had left unopened; a little later, however, when the Procureur Général read to the Grand'Chambre a letter from Bordeaux, the Enquêtes demanded assembly of the chambers to consider the two letters. The government then acted: on September 2nd the Regent summoned a delegation of the Parlement. They were reminded that the Court had agreed not to hold assemblies of the chambers during the year 1649,[4] and assured that the affairs of the two provinces would be satisfactorily attended to by the Council. The chambers were not assembled, but the Enquêtes commissioned two of their members to take charge of the interests of Guyenne and Provence during the recess, which was at hand.

Serious as the disorders in the provinces were, they were not the main concern of the government. The Prince of Condé, first Prince of the Blood, and the military genius of the age, had set himself in open opposition to the First Minister. In September this quarrel was already several months old. Its occasion had been the projected marriage between a niece of Mazarin and the oldest son of the Duke of Vendôme, the Duke of Mercoeur, the object of which alliance was to create a party among the grandees for the Minister, and to bring over to the government the Duke of Vendôme's second son, the Duke of Beaufort. News of these negotiations became public in April. Condé opposed the marriage as a *mésalliance* of the royal blood, and out of jealousy of the house of Vendôme, who were to be given a

---

[3] I have taken these facts from Chéruel, *Minorité de Louis XIV*, III, 240-243.

[4] The agreement had been verbal; we have seen that this clause in the Treaty of Rueil was revoked.

great prize, the Admiralty; he refused to accept command of the army on the northern front and retired to Burgundy, of which he was Governor. In August he came to Paris with the King, but maintained an attitude of hostile reserve toward the Minister.

The break came on the 14th of September. The marriage was about to be celebrated, and the Cardinal asked Condé for his consent. The Prince replied that his consent was not necessary, since he was not a relative (the Vendômes were illegitimate), and demanded that the Pont-de-l'Arche, an important fortress in Normandy, be given to his brother-in-law, the Duke of Longueville, in accordance with a promise which the Cardinal had made at the time of the peace negotiations after the blockade of Paris. Mazarin protested that the Prince had agreed that this promise would not be kept. Condé accused him of perfidy, and quit him with an insult which became immediately famous: "Adieu Mars!" The next day the Prince was waited on by a crowd of nobles, including the chiefs of the Fronde,[5] who offered their support against the Minister. It was reported that Condé would go to the Parlement and demand reënactment of the Decree of 1617.

Here was an alliance between the first Prince of the Blood and an important element of the opposition. The Minister was in a precarious position. He saved himself by a complete capitulation. Through the mediation of the Duke of Orleans a formal treaty was drawn, deposited with the First President of the Parlement, which gave Condé control of the government. The Minister promised "that he would not dispose of the governments, principal charges, and embassies, nor exile any person from the court, nor make any decision on any matter of importance to the state, except after having asked the Prince's advice; nor would he marry his nephew, nor his nieces, without having first consulted him." The Prince in return agreed "to further, in all ways possible, the reëstablishment of the authority of the

[5] According to Talon the term *frondeurs* was applied only to the intriguing element of the opposition, headed by Gondi and Beaufort. See his *Mémoires*, 383, 384, 391, 397, 432.

King in the position in which it had been before the last movements, and to serve the Cardinal as well in the interests of the
state as in his own personal interests, toward and against all
persons."[6] The engagement between the Cardinal's niece and
the Duke of Mercoeur was broken, and the promise of the
Admiralty to the Vendômes withdrawn.[7] Certain friends of
Condé were paid by the award of the honor of the *tabouret*,
that is, the right to sit in the presence of the Queen, to the
Princess of Marsillac and the Marquise de Pons. The Duke of
Longueville obtained satisfaction.

These acts, however, made the Prince many enemies, upon
whom the Minister could rest. The award of the *tabouret* to the
Princess of Marsillac and the Marquise de Pons raised the nobility against him, this honor being by tradition reserved to
Duchesses. In October a number of nobles met in Paris and
formed a league the purpose of which was "to do everything
compatible with the service of the King" to obtain revocation
of these awards; if any one of the associates should be injured
for cause of the league, the other members would support him
to death. They presented their petition to the Regent, which
she hastened to grant, glad of an excuse to retract favors which
had been extorted from her; also there was need of putting an
end to the assembly, which had turned to political matters: they
had begun to talk of taking steps to obtain assembly of the Estates General, elections for which had been held earlier in the
year.[8]

The Minister found stronger support in that clique of Frondeurs whom we saw for a moment associated with the Prince.
After he made his peace with Mazarin, they broke with him
noisily, accusing him of treachery. At the end of the year occurred an event which embittered this quarrel, and discredited
the Prince in Paris.

This was an involved and mysterious business. In the month
of November the *rentiers* of Paris began agitation for the pay-

---

[6] Bazin, *France*, I, 520.
[7] Talon, *Mémoires*, 365.
[8] Bazin, *France*, I, 532.

ment of the sums due them according to the arrangements made
at the end of the year 1648, and which the government, because
of the war, had been unable to carry out. A new *Surintendant*
of Finances, courting popularity, paid the amounts due. The
rentiers, however, secretly instigated by the Frondeurs, on the
pretext that no provision had been made for the future, held
assemblies and appointed syndics to take charge of their interests. At this the Parlement intervened. On December 4th a
conference between members of the Parlement and the *rentiers*
was held in the house of the First President, which ended in
confusion and disorder. Then, on the morning of December 11th,
it was reported to the Parlement that an attempt had been made
to assassinate one of the syndics of the *rentiers*, a certain Joly.
The chambers were immediately assembled. While they were in
session, the Marquis de la Boulaye, who was known to have
connections with the Frondeurs, arrived at the Palace of Justice
brandishing a pistol; he then rode through the city calling the
people to arms. The same evening, the affair was complicated
by another event: two carriages, one of which bore the arms of
the Prince of Condé, the other those of the Count of Duras,
were fired on while crossing the Pont-Neuf, and one of the
Count's servants was wounded. On December 14th the Prince
of Condé lodged a formal complaint with the Parlement.

The whole affair seemed highly suspicious, and the Court proceeded cautiously. It was soon clear that the pretended attempt
on Joly's life had been engineered by conspirators, and on December 19th the King's attorneys requested that he be prosecuted. Certain witnesses had testified against Beaufort, Broussel,
and Gondi, but this testimony was very doubtful. The government, however, insisted that they be put on trial, and the
Procureur Général concluded to this effect on December 22nd,
overriding the opposition of his two colleagues, who refused to
appear with him. The Parlement ordered them to defend
themselves.[9]

For a month the Court was occupied with this trial, the de-
fendants securing delays on various pretexts. During this time

---

[9] For these events see Talon, *Mémoires*, 368-373.

the Prince of Condé pursued his opponents vindictively, further alienating the people of Paris, who looked upon them as their champions, and had not forgotten that he had commanded the government's army in the blockade.

In the meantime relations between the Prince and the government had become further embittered. Condé advocated the cause of the rebels of Guyenne, where the quarrel between the Governor and the city had flamed up again.[10] He openly protected the Count of Jarzé, who had been disgraced for having pretended to the intimate favors of the Queen. Finally, he was responsible for the marriage of the Duke of Richelieu. This person, grandnephew of the former minister, and one of the richest lords of the kingdom, was still a minor. He had fallen violently in love with the Marquise de Pons, who was an intimate of Condé's sister, the Duchess of Longueville. The affair was encouraged by Condé and his family: among the Duke of Richelieu's possessions was the government of Le Havre, a very important fortress, the control of which would place Normandy completely in the power of the Duke of Longueville. In defiance of the opposition of the government and the young Duke's guardian, the marriage was celebrated on December 26th, in the presence of Condé, his brother Conti, and the Duchess of Longueville. The Duke of Richelieu shut himself up in Le Havre, and refused to receive an officer sent by the government to take command of the garrison.

Though by this time sure of the Frondeurs and the city, the government could not venture to take action against Condé without the support of the King's uncle, the Duke of Orleans, Lieutenant General of the Kingdom. He was jealous of the Prince, but was by nature indolent and timorous, and was completely dominated by his favorite, Abbé de la Rivière, who had been bought by Condé. Mazarin, in a masterpiece of intrigue, succeeded in discrediting Rivière with his master, and the Duke gave his consent to the imprisonment of Condé.[11] On January 18th Condé, Conti, and the Duke of Longueville were arrested

---

[10] Bazin, *France*, I, 524.
[11] Chéruel, *Minorité de Louis XIV*, III, 350-362.

in the Council chamber and taken to Vincennes. The event was celebrated with bonfires by the people of Paris.

2. THE FIRST WAR

On January 19th (1650), the day after the arrest of the Princes, the government explained their motives in a great Council, attended by a large number of lords, and a deputation from the Parlement. These were set forth at length in a *lettre de cachet* read to the Parlement on the 20th. This letter is criticized by the Advocate General in his memoirs as impolitic and weak. Government should never, Talon says, enter into details with subjects in regard to the *arcanum imperii*; also the King accused the Princes of no act which could properly be called criminal.[12]

The trial of Beaufort, Gondi, and Broussel was brought to a close two days later, with an acquittal. The party of the Fronde had been of material assistance to the Minister in the intrigues which had preceded the arrests, and received rich rewards in offices and money. With the appointment of Châteauneuf to the place of *Garde des Sceaux*, and of President de Maisons to the *Surintendance* of Finances, they entered the government, where they had considerable power through their influence over the Duke of Orleans.

The coup d'état immediately produced rebellions in the provinces: the friends of the Princes scattered to their governments and prepared to secure justice by force of arms. Mme. de Longueville went to Normandy, the Duke de la Rochefoucauld to Poitou, the Duke de Bouillon to Turenne, and his brother the Maréchal de Turenne, to his fortress Stenay, on the northern frontier. The Count of Tavannes attempted to raise Burgundy, the government of the Prince of Condé.

Normandy was dealt with first, and gave little trouble. The King and the Regent with a small army entered the province early in February, and left it entirely pacified at the end of three weeks: The Duchess of Longueville had taken ship for Holland, and the Duke of Richelieu, upon whom the rebels had

---

[12] Talon, *Mémoires*, 380.

counted for Le Havre, had made his submission. The court returned to Paris on February 21st, and on March 5th left for Burgundy.

There the situation seemed more serious. Dijon, the capital, had closed its gates to the rebels, but was by no means secure: when the new Governor, Vendôme, had ventured to criticize Condé in the Parlement, the First President replied that Burgundy had never had to complain of the government of the Princes of the house of Condé, and that saving the service of the King, all the inhabitants of the province were ready to sacrifice themselves for them.[13] The Count of Tavannes, with a considerable force, had shut himself up in the fortress of Bellegarde. Nevertheless the court entered Dijon on the 16th of March, and Tavannes surrendered Bellegarde on April 11th, after a short siege.

But the capital of the party of the Princes was Stenay. There, on April 20th, Turenne and Mme. de Longueville, who had joined him, concluded an alliance with the Spaniards, agreeing not to make peace with the government until the Princes had been released, and "a just, equal, and reasonable peace had been offered to Spain."[14] At the end of May a Spanish army crossed the frontier and was joined by Turenne, with a considerable force.

The French court took up residence at Compiègne on June 2nd, to be near the scene of military operations. On the tenth the enemy besieged le Câtelet, which surrendered at the end of a few days, and on the fifteenth they laid siege to Guise. Here, however, they met with stiff resistance, and were obliged to raise the siege on July 1st.

By this time, however, the court was in Paris, preparing for a journey to the other end of the kingdom. A situation had developed in Guyenne which seemed to require the immediate presence of the King and the government.

It was stated above that war between Bordeaux and the Duke d'Épernon had broken out again in the fall of 1649. The government had commissioned the Maréchal du Plessis to make peace,

[13] Chéruel, *Minorité de Louis XIV*, IV, 40-41.
[14] Bazin, *France*, II, 20.

but the city, which was preparing to rid itself of the Château Trompette, refused to admit him. The castle fell on October 18th. Du Plessis, who had been treated with scant respect, summoned a royal naval force from La Rochelle, but accomplished little. A declaration of the King in December gave satisfaction to the city in their other main grievance against the Governor, the fort at Libourne: it was ordered destroyed.[15]

Bordeaux and the Parlement, however, did not consider themselves secure while the government of the province was in the hands of the Duke d'Épernon, and would take the first opportunity to reopen hostilities. On May 31st the city opened its gates to the Prince of Condé's wife and his young son, who had been escorted across country from Turenne by a small army led by La Rochefoucauld and Bouillon. On June 1st the Parlement of Bordeaux decreed that the King should be petitioned to send the Princes before their natural judges, and to allow the Princess of Condé and her son to remain in the city; on the 18th they addressed a letter to the Parlement of Paris, demanding aid, and on the 25th they declared war on the Duke d'Épernon. Early in July they attempted to keep the rebellion within bounds by voting to investigate the arrival of a Spanish agent at the house of the Princess of Condé, but they were mobbed by an infuriated crowd and probably saved from injury by the intervention of the Princess. On July 28th, at the approach of the King and the government, they threatened to renew the decree of 1617, against Mazarin.[16]

The court established itself at Libourne on the first of August, and there received a delegation from the Parlement of Bordeaux, who were given a declaration offering amnesty to all except the lords who had negotiated with Spain. The Parlement deliberated on this declaration August 6th and 7th. But then occurred an event which made a peaceful solution impossible. The commander of the government's army, Marshal de la Meilleraye, laid siege to the château of Vayres, on the Dordogne, which was garrisoned by soldiers of the city commanded by a certain

[15] Chéruel, *Minorité de Louis XIV*, IV, 120, Note 1.
[16] Bazin, *France*, II, 35.

Richon. The garrison rebelled. Richon was taken, tried, and hanged in Libourne. The Princess of Condé immediately assembled a council of the generals and the city authorities, who decided on reprisal. One of their prisoners, the Baron de Canol, was hanged.

Several weeks passed before the government was ready to attack the city in earnest. Finally, on September 5th, the royal army advanced on the suburb Saint-Surin, defended by the Dukes of Bouillon and La Rochefoucauld, which they took, but with heavy losses. The gate which was their objective, the Porte Dijeaux, was still covered by a fortification. For ten days the government's forces struggled to capture this fortification without success. On September 16th the Regent granted an armistice, and peace negotiations began.

The mediators in the negotiations between the government and the city were delegates from the Parlement of Paris.

It will have been noticed that the great Court has thus far figured very little in our narrative of the events which followed the arrest of the Princes. Until the outbreak in Guyenne, they had, in fact, given the government little trouble. At the end of April, when the Dowager Princess of Condé had presented herself in the Parlement as a supplicant for her sons, they had refused to entertain her petition, though treating her with the greatest respect. In May they had registered declarations of treason against Mme. de Longueville, Bouillon, Turenne, and La Rochefoucauld, and had taken action against two conspirators in Paris of the party of the Princes, Matha and Fontrailles, who were accused of attempting to form a league of nobles, and of having drafted a petition for the assembly of the Estates General.[17] Early in July, however, having received a delegate from the Parlement of Bordeaux, they decided to intervene. On July 7th, overriding the request of the Advocate General, who, in a careful speech, had urged that such matters were of the *arcanum imperii*, and outside the jurisdiction of the Court,[18] they voted to send a deputation to the Regent with a petition urging that

[17] Talon, *Mémoires*, 390.
[18] Talon, *Mémoires*, 391.

she listen with kindness to the complaints of the Parlement of Bordeaux. Through the summer opposition sentiment grew steadily in strength, despite the resistance of the Duke of Orleans, who represented the government in Paris. Early in August the chambers were again assembled on the affairs of Bordeaux; on the eighth it was proposed, but not carried, that remonstrances be made to the Regent for the liberty of the Princes; at this session President Viole urged that action be taken against Mazarin. On September 5th a new deputation was ordered to go to the Regent, on the 7th the Parlement was continued into the recess for public affairs, and on the 12th, in a test vote, the government obtained a majority of only nine: 73 to 64.[19]

In Paris, then, the government's position was none too secure. They hastened to make peace with Bordeaux. To obtain it they had to make great sacrifices. They refused to concede the liberty of the Princes, but granted a complete amnesty for the rebellion, and promised not to restore the Duke d'Épernon, who had been ordered from the province some time before.[20] These terms were formally accepted by the Parlement of Bordeaux on October 2nd.

After a sojourn of a few days in Bordeaux, the court took its way northward, arriving at Fontainebleau on the 8th of November, where they stopped, not venturing to enter Paris until they had made sure of the disposition of the Duke of Orleans, who, in the past month, had seemed to incline toward the opposition. The Duke, having been begged and reassured, finally consented to come to Fontainebleau on November 10th. The government wrested from him his consent to the transfer of the Princes from the château of Marcoussis to Le Havre, where they would be out of reach of the conspirators in Paris, and in the control of the Minister. The Regent and the ministers entered Paris without ceremony on November 15th; the same day the Princes, under heavy guard, started for Le Havre, where they arrived on the 25th.

In the capital, as a result of the failure in Guyenne, the presence of foreign troops in the northern provinces, and the constant

---

[19] Talon, *Mémoires*, 397.
[20] Bazin, *France*, II, 67-71.

agitation of the Frondeurs and the party of the Princes, the credit of the government had sunk low. On October 29th[21] Beaufort's carriage had been attacked by eight or ten men, and one of the gentlemen of his suite killed. Mazarin was accused of responsibility for this act in a pamphlet, *Les dernières finesses du Mazarin*, and hanged in effigy. The Minister determined to reëstablish himself by a feat of arms.

After the departure of the court to Guyenne, the Spaniards and Turenne had scored considerable successes in Champagne and Picardy. La Capelle was captured in July; in August they took Rethel and Château-Porcien, and Turenne defeated the main government force, under Hocquincourt, near Fismes. This victory opened the road to Paris. The Duke of Orleans, highly alarmed, took measures for the defence of the capital, and moved the Princes from Vincennes to Marcoussis. Turenne and the Spaniards withdrew, but left garrisons in the captured towns. Of these, Rethel was very important, capable of holding 6,000 men, and so situated as to dominate the communications of the capital with a section of the frontier.[22]

Mazarin decided to attack this place. On December 9th the siege was begun by Marshal du Plessis, who was joined presently by the Minister. It fell on the 13th, when Turenne, who was marching to its relief, was only a short distance away. Du Plessis then turned against Turenne, succeeded in tempting him into a battle, and defeated him decisively on December 15th. Mazarin returned to Paris on the last day of the month.

His victory had availed him nothing: the day before his return, December 30th, the Parlement, after long debates, had decreed that the Regent should be petitioned to release the Princes. The struggle between the government and the opposition, made up of the most diverse elements, had already been going on for a month. It lasted five weeks longer, and ended in the release of the Princes, and the exile of the Minister.

The Parlement presented their remonstrances on January 20th,

---

[21] I take this date from Bazin, *France*, II, 86. Talon gives it as November 29, but this is doubtless an error.

[22] Chéruel, *Minorité de Louis XIV*, IV, 187.

the Regent having obtained this delay on the pretext of illness. The First President, who spoke for the Parlement, used strong language: "If one compares," said Molé, "the misfortunes which have happened since the eighteenth of January, 1650, with the preceding conduct of affairs, it is easy to pronounce judgment on that unfortunate policy (*cette politique infortunée*) which is the cause of all our ills, for since that fatal and unhappy day we have had nothing but divided minds, civil wars, and decline of the royal authority. Your Majesties have been in perpetual anxiety." He requested that the Princes be released so that they could continue "to furnish proofs of their worth."[23] The government met this move by agreeing to work toward the release of the Princes as soon as Turenne, Mme. de Longueville, and the other rebels had laid down their arms. The Court probably would have stopped here, but on February 4th occurred an event which forced the Regent to yield: the Duke of Orleans demanded the dismissal of Mazarin.

This was mainly the work of that group of intriguers, directed by Gondi, who had been largely responsible for the arrest of the Princes. Though rewarded by the Minister, they had continued to oppose him, attempting to control the government through their influence over the Duke of Orleans. This opposition, at first concealed, became open shortly after the campaign in Guyenne, when the government refused Gondi nomination to the cardinalate.[24] The Fronde then joined forces with the party of the Princes. A formal treaty was drawn up between the two parties, the contractants agreeing to use their influence to obtain the Duke of Orleans' support for the release of the Princes and the dismissal of Mazarin. The Duke yielded on January 30th, signing a treaty with the new party in which he promised to act for the Princes and against the Minister. In return, the Princes, through their representatives, agreed to allow the Duke to control the Council.[25]

Action followed immediately. On the evening of February 1st,

[23] Talon, *Mémoires*, 405-406.
[24] Chéruel, *Minorité de Louis XIV*, IV, 195.
[25] Chéruel, *Minorité de Louis XIV*, IV, 250.

at the Palais Royal, there was a sharp dispute between Orleans
and the Cardinal. Mazarin said that the nobility and the people
were hostile to the monarchy, and compared the leaders of the
opposition to Fairfax and Cromwell. The Duke replied that the
monarchy was not in question, but only the bad government of
the Minister.[26] The next day the Duke announced that he would
not attend the Council so long as Mazarin was a member. On
February 3rd Gondi informed the Parlement of the Duke's intention, and repeated Mazarin's words at the Palais Royal. On
the fourth Orleans, in the Parlement, spoke at length and with
great force against the Cardinal, and on the same day it was
decreed that the Regent should be very humbly petitioned to
issue *lettres de cachet* immediately for the release of the Princes,
and to remove the Cardinal from the Council and the proximity
of the King. On the night of February 6th Mazarin quit Paris
in disguise, and five days later messengers started for Le Havre
with letters ordering the release of the Princes, who entered Paris
in triumph on the sixteenth.

3. CONDÉ AND THE REGENT

Mazarin was dismissed, but there was no assurance that he
would not some time be recalled. To provide against this, and
also, doubtless, to obtain an advantage over their old enemies,
the clergy, the Parlement, on February 7th, petitioned the
Regent for a declaration "excluding in the future from the councils of the King all foreigners, even naturalized, and others who
shall have sworn an oath to a prince other than the King."[27]
This move produced a sharp controversy, which lasted for two
months.

The Parlement was opposed by the *Garde des Sceaux*, Châteauneuf, who aspired to the cardinalate and the first place in
the Council, by the clique of the Fronde, whose leader Gondi
had the same ambitions, and finally by the whole body of the
clergy. On February 20th the declaration demanded by the

[26] Talon, *Mémoires*, 407; Chéruel, *Minorité de Louis XIV*, 255-256.
[27] Talon, *Mémoires*, 412.
Mazarin had been naturalized.

Parlement was presented by the King's attorneys, but was rejected as not being sufficiently explicit; the King was petitioned to declare that he would not employ French cardinals in his Council. On March 1st the declaration was returned to the Parlement, revised, but still without mention of the French cardinals. The next day the Court decreed that the Regent should be petitioned to change it in accordance with their wishes. This request was presented on March 15th by the Advocate General, who defended the cause of the Court in a remarkable speech. Cardinals, Talon said, were unfit for the ministry because the interests of the Pope, both as head of the Church and temporal prince, must be their first concern, and because by papal legislation they were not subject to the jurisdiction of the King.[28] The Regent replied evasively.

On March 18th the affair was complicated by the intervention of the Assembly of the Clergy, who petitioned the *Garde des Sceaux* against the declaration, which they characterized as "an innovation tending directly toward overturning the three orders of the kingdom, by weakening the one which had always held the first rank, which was entirely contrary to the honor of the Church, the service of the King, and the good of the state."[29] The Parlement objected violently to the language of this petition. On March 27th the First President asked the Duke of Orleans to use his influence with the Regent to obtain the declaration, which was more necessary than ever since the Clergy had accused the Court, "the first company of the Kingdom," of acting against the interest of the King and the state. Two days later the Duke and the Prince of Condé went to the *Garde des Sceaux*, who had announced his opposition to the declaration. Châteauneuf persisted in his refusal, asserting that the King could not make laws during his minority, and that he would give up his office rather than consent to an act which was nothing short of cowardice. On March 30th the King's attorneys were again sent to the Regent; Talon fortified his earlier arguments

[28] Talon, *Mémoires*, 419-422. The speech is quoted in part in Chapter III.
[29] Talon, *Mémoires*, 422.
The Assembly of the Clergy had been in session since May 15th, 1650.

by citing a recent papal bull which ordered that all cardinals should reside in Rome. The Regent again refusing to answer definitely, the Parlement voted to send a deputation with remonstrances. Audience was granted the deputation on April 3rd; Molé, speaking for the Parlement, requested the declaration, which, he said, could not be objected to, since it had been approved in the Parlement by the Duke of Orleans and the Prince of Condé. The Regent promised to modify the declaration as requested. This was done, and the declaration was registered by the Parlement on April 20th.

This controversy had been interrupted for a time in March by another, which seemed more serious. Shortly after the Duke of Orleans' break with the government, a number of nobles under the patronage of the Duke had formed an association in Paris to obtain the release of the Princes and the dismissal of Mazarin, who, they asserted, had insulted the whole body of the nobility of France by his remarks at the Palais Royal. These objects having been obtained, the association continued their meetings, demanding assembly of the Estates General. They were encouraged in this by the Duke of Orleans, influenced by Gondi, who had formed the project of postponing the majority of the King by the authority of the Estates.[30] By the beginning of March the Assembly of the Nobility, as it was called, had assumed dangerous proportions, numbering eight hundred or a thousand persons. They sought support from the Assembly of the Clergy, and were successful: on March 15th that body voted to join them in their demand for the Estates General.

The pressure was now great, and on March 16th the Regent promised the Estates, but for October 1st, which would be some three weeks after the majority of the King; the Assembly of the Nobility was ordered to disperse. The Assembly continued to meet, demanding that the Estates be convoked before the King's majority.

The Parlement then intervened. Earlier in the month the Enquêtes had demanded an investigation; when this was reported to the Assembly of the Nobility, violent language had been used

---

[30] Talon, *Mémoires*, 423.

against the Court, and especially the First President and his son.
On March 20th, in the Parlement, the First President complained
in general terms of the menaces of the Assembly, and it was
ordered that the Duke of Orleans should be requested to take
his place in the Court. He came on the 23rd, and attempted to
avoid the question by complaining that the Regent was still
dominated by Mazarin through his creatures in the Council,
Servien, Lyonne, and Le Tellier, and that it was their intention
to obtain the recall of the Cardinal at the majority of the King.
Molé refused to listen, insisting that the Duke, who was responsible for the Assembly, should order them to disperse; otherwise
the Parlement would take action. The Duke demanded and
obtained three days delay. The next day, March 24th, the
Regent advanced the date of the assembly of the Estates to
September 8th, the day after the majority was to be declared.
This response was given in writing, signed by the King, the
Regent, and the four Secretaries of State; besides promising the
Estates, this document gave permission to the Duke of Orleans
and the Prince of Condé to assemble the nobility in case the
Estates were not convoked precisely on the date indicated. The
following day Orleans and Condé went to the Assembly of the
Clergy and the Assembly of the Nobility and left with them a
statement embodying the Regent's response, and their own
promise to do everything in their power to have it executed.
On March 27th the Duke of Orleans announced to the Parlement
the separation of the Assembly of the Nobility.[31]

Though apparently successful in the matter of the Estates,
the Regent had in fact possessed little power since Mazarin's
flight. She had plotted to escape from Paris with the King and
join the Minister,[32] who waited several days at St. Germain,
and did not leave the kingdom until the middle of March. This
project was defeated by the watchfulness of the opposition. On
February 9th the Parlement ordered that the Cardinal, his relatives and servants, should quit the kingdom within fifteen days, on
penalty of outlawry. The same night the rumor spread that the

[31] *Iournal de l'assemblée de la noblesse etc.*
[32] Chéruel, *Minorité de Louis XIV*, IV, 271; Talon, *Mémoires*, 413.

Regent was planning to leave, and the streets were patrolled until morning by troops of the Duke of Orleans. The next day the Regent swore to the King's attorneys, who had been sent by the Parlement, that she had never intended to go out of Paris, and ordered that the gates be guarded. She was taken at her word, and for several weeks the King and the Regent were practically prisoners in the Palais Royal, Talon says, *in libera custodia.*[33]

Until the beginning of April the government was in the hands of the Duke of Orleans, or rather of the Frondeurs who dominated him, notably Gondi and Mme. de Chevreuse. In the Council the *Garde des Sceaux*, Châteauneuf, held the first place. The Prince of Condé, tied by the engagements he had been obliged to make to get out of prison, played a secondary rôle. He was not made for such a part, and Mazarin, who was in constant communication with the Regent from his refuge in the Bishopric of Liège,[34] saw that he could use him to break up the alliance of the two parties which had brought about his disgrace. On April 3rd the Regent performed a coup d'état: without consulting the Duke of Orleans, she dismissed Châteauneuf, and called to the Council three friends of Condé, Chavigny, Séguier, and the First President of the Parlement, who was given the seals. The Fronde immediately held a council at the Luxembourg, attended by Condé, in which violent proposals were put forward; Condé, however, appearing luke-warm, these were abandoned, and the Duke of Orleans contented himself with the dismissal on April 14th of Molé, the most objectionable of the appointees.

Shortly afterward, an act of Condé's family, for which the Duchess of Longueville was largely responsible, envenomed the hatred of the Fronde. One of the provisions of the treaty between the two parties had been the marriage of the Prince of Conti and the daughter of Mme. de Chevreuse. This had been hard for the Condés to accept, because it would place Conti in

[33] The gates were guarded until March 30th. *Journal du Parlement*, March 30.

[34] Mazarin went to Brühl in the Electorate of Cologne on April 11th, where he remained until the end of October. Chéruel, *Minorité de Louis XIV*, IV, 289.

the control of the Orleans group, and because Mlle. de Chevreuse had been dishonored by a notorious liaison with Gondi. In the middle of April this engagement was broken. The Fronde immediately opened negotiations with Mazarin.[35]

These negotiations did not immediately produce results, and until July Condé was all powerful. He used his position to entrench himself solidly. Important fortresses were distributed among his friends; he himself, in exchange for Burgundy, obtained the government of Guyenne, which had already proved its devotion to him and his family, and was in easy reach of assistance from Spain. He then demanded Provence for his brother Conti, which, with Guyenne, would enable him to dominate the whole southern part of the kingdom. The Regent, counselled by Mazarin, steadily refused the demand for Provence.

By the end of June the coalition of the Fronde and the friends of the Cardinal was ready for action. Several conferences were held between the Regent, Gondi, and the Duchess de Chevreuse, in which a project of arresting Condé in the palace of the Duke of Orleans was discussed. This had to be abandoned because of the opposition of Orleans. Then, it is said, in a council of the Fronde, attended by one of the ministers, Lyonne, it was proposed to attack Condé in the streets of Paris, and even to kill him.[36] Information of this project reached Condé indirectly from Lyonne. He was on his guard. On the night of July 5th, learning that there were suspicious movements of troops in the city, he threw himself on a horse and rode to Saint-Maur, part of the way across the fields.

The Prince was now convinced that there was no peace with the Regent. Two months of negotiations and intrigues followed, which served only to embitter him further, and ended finally in an open break and a new civil war. Immediately after his flight to Saint-Maur he appealed to the Parlement through his brother Conti, and by letter, justifying his departure on grounds of the information he had received of the project to arrest him for the second time, and declaring that he could never feel secure

---

[35] Chéruel, *Minorité de Louis XIV*, IV, 327.
[36] Chéruel, *Minorité de Louis XIV*, IV, 361-362; Bazin, *France*, II, 149.

as long as the Regent was dominated by the agents of Mazarin in the Council. The Parlement, influenced by Molé, delayed action for several days, but finally, on July 14th, decreed that a delegation should be sent to the Regent to ask for a declaration which would give assurance that Mazarin would never be recalled to the ministry. The Regent promised this declaration on the eighteenth, and on the 20th informed the Parlement that Servien, Le Tellier, and Lyonne, Mazarin's creatures in the Council, had been dismissed.

Condé returned to Paris, but refused to pay his respects to the King and the Regent, and continued his proceedings against Mazarin. On August 2nd the Parlement decreed that the conspiracy against Condé should be investigated, that the Regent's promise not to recall Mazarin should be entered on the register, and that the Duke of Mercoeur, whose secret marriage to one of Mazarin's nieces had become known, should take his place in the Parlement.[37]

But the Regent had now made final arrangements with the Fronde, promising Gondi the cardinalate,[38] and, with this support, determined to act. On the seventeenth of August she convoked an assembly of great lords, delegates of the Sovereign Courts and the city government, and had read to them a statement of the griefs of the King against Condé, who was accused among other things of conspiring with Spain, and withdrawing his and his brother's troops from the royal armies; the statement ended with a threat: "the King would employ the means which God had placed in his hands to prevent these pernicious designs and arrest their course."[39]

This move had been approved by the Duke of Orleans, but he was timid, and could not stand against Condé. On the nineteenth he sent a letter to the Parlement which exonerated the Prince, and on September 4th the Parlement requested a declaration of the latter's innocence, which would be solemnly published at the *lit de justice*, three days later, when the King's

[37] *Journal du Parlement*, at this date.
[38] Chéruel, *Minorité de Louis XIV*, IV, 387-390.
[39] Bazin, *France*, II, 163.

majority was to be declared.[40] On September 6th the declaration against Mazarin was published, which had been promised in July, and the following day, at the *lit de justice*, the declaration of Condé's innocence.

But the Prince was not present at the *lit de justice:* he had left Paris the evening of the sixth.[41]

4. THE SECOND WAR

Immediately after the declaration of the King's majority, the Regent took the offensive against Condé, calling to the Council three of his enemies: Châteauneuf, La Vieuville, and Molé. After this act the Prince, who had remained near Paris in hope of a peaceful solution, went to Montrond in Bourbonnais. There he took counsel with the leaders of his party, the Duchess of Longueville, Conti, Nemours, and La Rochefoucauld, and decided upon war. On September 22nd he arrived at Bordeaux, capital of his government, and was received like a sovereign.

The adventure upon which he had embarked seemed by no means desperate. He was a great commander, and had at his disposal important resources. He could count on the support of Guyenne; he had an army on the northern frontier under a man whom he could trust, Tavannes, and fortresses in Burgundy, Bourbonnais, Berri. The foreign enemy of the government, Spain, would certainly send him aid, and there was possibility of help from England.

He determined to keep the fighting at a distance from Guyenne. By November he had cleared the province of government troops, and had made considerable progress in Angoumois and Saintonge. In the middle of that month, however, he was defeated.

[40] According to Talon, in his speech at the *lit de justice*, this expression is incorrect: "What was done at Rouen in the year 1563, and by imitation in this Court in the year 1614, and the ceremony in which we are engaged to-day, are not declarations of majority, but rather public acts performed by a major King." Talon, *Mémoires*, 442.

[41] A passage in a letter of Mazarin to the Queen implies that Condé suspected, with reason, that he would be arrested immediately after the majority of the King. *Lettres à la Reine*, 318.

The government, having decided on energetic action, had quit Paris at the end of September, and after a short stay at Fontainbleau, proceeded to Bourges, which had been occupied by the Prince of Conti. The inhabitants of this place opened their gates to the King on October 8th; the citadel, the Grosse Tour, was taken shortly afterward, and destroyed. On October 31st the court took up residence at Poitiers, to be near the center of operations. At this moment Condé looked extremely dangerous: he had occupied La Rochelle, and had laid siege to Cognac. But on November 17th the royal commander, Harcourt, defeated the Prince's army before Cognac, and at the end of the month regained control of La Rochelle.

This success improved the position of the government, but then occurred an event which gave new strength to the rebellion. This was the return of Mazarin. In October he left Brühl, and went to Huy, close to the frontier, where he started to collect an army of German mercenaries. On the twenty-fourth of December, after issuing a manifesto declaring that he was acting in obedience to the command of the King, he entered Sedan. Thence, with about 5,000 of his own troops, and 2,000 of the King's, commanded by Hocquincourt, he marched to Poitiers to join the court, where he arrived on January 28th, 1652, and was received with the greatest honors.

The government's intention of recalling Mazarin became known in Paris in November. A declaration against Condé and his adherents had been sent to the Parlement in October. At the end of November the government brought pressure to have it registered through the First President and *Garde des Sceaux*, Molé, who had remained in Paris. The Court, informed by the Duke of Orleans on November 23rd that Mazarin had received a passport to return to France, proceeded very deliberately. The declaration was finally registered on December 4th, but with the amendment that the Princes of the Blood must be tried in full Parlement with the King present, and the others according to law; on the same day it was ordered that the activities of Mazarin should be investigated.[42] On December 13th the Parle-

[42] *Journal du Parlement*, December 4.

ment decreed that a deputation should go to the King with remonstrances: he should be petitioned to give his word that he intended to maintain the declaration against Mazarin which had been published on September 6th, and to dismiss the Cardinal's adherents from the Council; the decree added that the other Parlements should be invited to pass like decrees. The King, by *lettre de cachet*, forbade the deputation, and on the twenty-seventh of December the representatives of the government, Molé and La Vieuville, withdrew from the capital. At the same time Mazarin's invasion became certain. On the twenty-ninth the Parlement passed a decree of outlawry against him, and put a price of 150,000 livres on his head, to be furnished by the sale of his library; the Duke of Orleans was to be begged to employ "the King's authority and his own" to enforce the declaration of the King and the decrees of the Parlement against Mazarin.[43]

But the most serious consequence of the return of Mazarin was the definite defection of the Duke of Orleans. On January 24th a treaty was signed by agents of the Duke and the Prince of Condé, the contractants agreeing not to lay down their arms until Mazarin had been driven from the country, to have the Estates General convoked at Paris or a neighboring town, to obtain the exclusion of La Vieuville from the Council, and to work toward peace with Spain.[44] Action followed immediately. The government sent their main army to besiege Angers, which had been drawn into the revolt by the Duke of Rohan; Orleans, who had withdrawn his troops from the King's army, sent them to the relief of the town, under the command of Beaufort. Rohan capitulated (February 28) before Beaufort reached him, but this reverse was more than made up in the middle of March, when Beaufort was joined near Chartres by the Duke of Nemours with the Prince of Condé's northern army, reinforced with a corps of Spaniards. In the south, in the meantime, Condé, who

[43] Talon, *Mémoires*, 459-460.

Talon says this decree was severely criticized, both for the putting of a price on Mazarin's head, and for the authority given the Duke of Orleans: "the King being major, he was no longer Lieutenant General of the State and had in the Kingdom no other authority than his birth."

[44] Chéruel, *Ministère de Mazarin*, I, 105-106.

was outnumbered, and whose army was made up of raw recruits, had barely held his own against the government forces.

Simultaneously with this struggle in the field there was in progress another, more important conflict, in the Parlement of Paris. After the decree of December 29th against Mazarin, it seemed that the Court would stop at nothing; but on January 10th they declined to accede to the Duke of Orleans' request to order that the money in the public treasury should be seized and used to raise an army. On the eleventh, however, they decreed that the declaration against Condé should be suspended until the one against Mazarin was executed,[45] and when Nemours marched south with his Spaniards and the Prince of Condé's army, they refused to intervene, though ordered to do so by two *lettres de cachet*.[46]

The Parlement seemed to tremble in the balance. Condé thought that his presence might be decisive. On March 23rd he left Agen with eight or nine companions, and reached the outposts of Beaufort's and Nemours' army at Lorris in Gâtinais on April 1st, an incredibly rapid journey. On the seventh, with these troops, he defeated the royal army at Bleneau, and on the eleventh entered Paris.

For the three following months the Prince labored to bring the Parlement to pronounce definitely in his favor, employing all methods except open coercion, but without success.

When he took his place in the Court on April 12th, he was severely reprimanded by President Le Bailleul; however, the following day, despite letters patent ordering suspension of the declaration against Mazarin, a decree was passed which ordered that the King should be petitioned to dismiss him, that the other Parlements should be invited to pass like decrees, and that an assembly of the authorities of the capital should be held to listen to the Princes. This assembly, which met on April 19th, refused to go farther than the Parlement, voting (April 22) that remonstrances should be presented to the King against Mazarin, but also that the city would not join the Princes, and would not

[45] *Journal du Parlement*, January 12.
[46] Talon, *Mémoires*, 469.

furnish money to raise troops.[47] Condé then tried action with
volunteers from the city against the King's troops, capturing
Saint-Denis on May 11th. Still the Court and the capital refused to move. The mob was then called in. Already, on April
2nd and 3rd, when news of the Prince's arrival had reached the
city, there had been serious disorders, which the Parlement had
punished by executions. After the attack on Saint-Denis there
were violent manifestations against the Court; Le Bailleul's
carriage was attacked. Orleans then asked the Parlement for
authority to keep order, which was given him (May 14), but
informally, without a discussion, and without a vote.

The government attempted to separate the Parlement from
the Princes, as they had done in 1649, by offering to treat with
the Court: on June 4th the King ordered that a deputation be
sent him with full powers. Stronger pressure was then brought
by the Princes. On June 21st, when the Court passed through
the hall of the Palace of Justice, they were jostled by a mob and
one of the judges was struck. The day of June 25th was terrible:
the judges were fired on as they left the Palace; none was
wounded, but, Talon says, it was a miracle, for men fell at their
sides. Nine days later came the massacre of the Hôtel de Ville.

This event was preceded by a bloody battle at the gates of
Paris. After the departure of Condé, the army of the Princes
had been shut up in Étampes by that of the King, commanded
by Turenne. They were defeated on May 4th, and were in serious danger until relieved by an invasion of the free lance Duke
of Lorraine, then in the pay of Spain (June 6). They left Étampes
and went to Saint-Cloud. This position became untenable at the
end of June, and on July 1st Condé started to move them to
Charenton, skirting the walls of the city. The next morning,
before this movement was completed, he was attacked in the
faubourg Saint-Antoine by Turenne. The fighting was desperate; Condé was outnumbered and probably would have been
crushed, had not the gates of the city opened to receive his
army. This was the act of the Duke of Orleans, who, after hesi-

[47] Talon, *Mémoires*, 478.

tating for several hours, finally gave the order to the city government.[48]

The Prince had been saved by the city in defiance of the command of the King. Condé was now master of Paris. He used his advantage to establish a revolutionary government. On July 4th, at the Hôtel de Ville, was held an assembly of delegates of all the public bodies of the capital, the clergy, the Courts, the city government, etc. Condé and Orleans presented themselves, thanked the city for their assistance, and declared that they would lay down their arms when the King had dismissed Mazarin. The Governor of the city, and the head of the city government, in reply, made no mention of alliance with the Princes. The Prince and the Duke left, and the Hôtel de Ville was immediately fired upon from the square, which was jammed with a mob, among whom were a number of soldiers in disguise. The assembly was besieged until late at night, when Beaufort finally intervened. About thirty had been killed or badly wounded, among them several supporters of the Princes. Two days later, the head of the city government having resigned, Broussel was elected to his place; on July 26th, the Parlement, by a vote of 74 to 69, decreed that the Duke of Orleans should be begged to take the quality of Lieutenant General throughout the kingdom, and Condé the command of the armies under his authority, in order to free the King from the captivity in which he was held by Cardinal Mazarin.[49] Orleans appointed a council of great lords, members of the Courts, and the Chancellor, Séguier.

These, however, were acts of desperation. After July 4th the Princes' cause was doomed. The Parlement which bowed to their will was acting under coercion; many of its most respected members had left Paris or refrained from attendance. The government completed their ruin by a judicious mixture of acts of

---

[48] The decision of the Paris government to come to Condé's aid was doubtless influenced by the presence of a furious mob in the Place de Grève. See the *Registres de l'Hôtel de Ville*, III, 40-41.

[49] Talon, *Mémoires*, 500.

The *Journal du Parlement* at the date July 26 has an interesting speech by Bignon, Advocate General, on the authority of the Duke of Orleans. It will be discussed in Chapter III.

authority and concessions. On August 6th the Parlement received an order transferring the Court to Pontoise; the same day, this declaration was registered at Pontoise in an assembly made up of Peers and refugees from the Parlement of Paris.[50] On August 12th the King replied to remonstrances of the Parlement of Pontoise by promising to dismiss Mazarin; this response, however, contained a panegyric of the Cardinal. Mazarin quit the court for Bouillon, on the frontier.

This was the beginning of the end. On September 3rd the Cour des Aides and the Chambre des Comptes replied to an order of translation by voting that they would cease exercise of their offices. On September 26th, the Duke of Orleans, intimidated by an assembly of royalists at the Palais Royal, granted passports to deputies of the six *corps des marchands* to visit the King, and on the thirteenth of October the Prince of Condé, who had been seriously ill for several weeks, left Paris for his army, which had been joined some time before by the troops of the Duke of Lorraine. Louis XIV entered Paris on October 21st, and the following day the Duke of Orleans quit the city.

The Parlement of Paris was involved in the destruction of the party of the Princes, losing much of what had been gained in 1648-1649. At a *lit de justice* held in the Louvre on October 22nd several judges were excluded from the amnesty and exiled, and the Court was forbidden "hereafter to take cognizance of the general affairs of the state and the direction of the finances, and to order or undertake anything against those who had the administration of these matters, under penalty of disobedience."[51] On December 31st the King came to the Palace of Justice and had thirteen fiscal edicts registered in his presence.[52] Mazarin entered Paris in triumph on February 3rd, 1653.

With the loss of Paris the fate of the Princes was sealed. Nevertheless the struggle continued for several months in the

[50] This declaration is an interesting statement of absolutistic doctrine. It is discussed in Chapter III.

[51] *Journal du Parlement*, at this date.

[52] Talon, *Mémoires*, 516.

Omer Talon died on December 25th, 1652. His narrative is continued from September 9th, 1652 to May, 1653 by his son, who succeeded him in his office.

provinces. Condé, who became in November generalissimo of the armies of Spain, though soon deprived of the Duke of Orleans' troops, took a number of towns on the northern frontier; several of these, however, were recaptured in December and January. One by one he lost the places which he held in the kingdom. Montrond had fallen at the end of the summer; Provence, where a serious revolt had broken out on Mazarin's invasion, in January, 1652, was reduced to submission in October. Bellegarde, the Prince's last fortress in Burgundy, capitulated on June 7th, 1653. Bordeaux, the seat of his power, held out until August. There his brother and sister had maintained themselves by help from Spain and an alliance with a popular faction known as the Ormée; they had purged the Parlement, and instituted a reign of terror. The royalist generals, Vendôme and Candale, the latter the son of the Duke d'Épernon, entered the city on August 3rd, 1653. One of the chiefs of the Ormée, the butcher Duretête, was broken on the wheel.

CHAPTER III

DECLARATIONS OF THE PUBLIC AUTHORITIES

THE events of the Fronde, as described above, indicate that this was a movement against the royal authority mainly in defense of the power of other authorities of the state. It has also appeared that the government and the opponents of the government justified their acts by appealing to different concepts of the form of the kingdom. But the movement cannot be comprehended without knowledge of these concepts. This we shall attempt to obtain from an analysis of the official declarations, and from the works written in defense of the parties. In this chapter we shall deal with the official declarations, starting with those of the opposition.

1. DECLARATIONS OF THE OPPOSITION

In the first phase of the Fronde, the main issue was the authority of the Sovereign Courts. Examination of their pronouncements reveals that they laid claim to independent authority,[1] a share in the government of the state.

Their right to independent jurisdictions is affirmed in the seventeenth of the twenty-seven articles drawn up by the Assembly of the Chambre St. Louis. It reads in part as follows: "Articles 91, 92, 97, 98, and 99 of the Ordinance of Blois shall be executed; accordingly all matters of contentious nature (*qui gisent en matière contentieuse*) shall be sent back to the Parlement and other Sovereign Courts to whom cognizance of these matters belongs by the ordinances, and they cannot be taken away from them by special commissions. . . ."[2] The King had encroached

---

[1] In Chapters V and VI we shall see that the word *independent* is commonly used in the defense of the opposition to describe the authority of the Sovereign Courts.

[2] The text of the Twenty-seven Articles is given in Isambert, XVII, 72-84.

upon the jurisdictions of the Sovereign Courts through the agency
of the royal Council and special commissions. By the last phrase
quoted the use of special commissions for this purpose is forbidden; by the articles cited in the Ordinance of Blois, the jurisdiction of the royal Council is definitely limited. The most
important of these, Article 97, reads: "We have declared and
declare that we do not intend in the future to accord (*bailler*)
any letters of evocation either general or particular, of our own
movement, but will that the requests of those who pursue the
said evocations be reported in our Privy Council by the regular
Maîtres des Requêtes of our Hôtel, who shall be in function, there
to be judged according to the Edicts of Bourdaisière and Chan-
teloup and other Edicts made subsequently by the Kings our
predecessors, and by us. . . ."[3]

Limiting thus in their favor the direct jurisdiction of the King,
the Assembly of the Chambre St. Louis attempted to provide
guaranties. In Article 1 they affirmed the right of the Courts to
sanction all extraordinary commissions. It reads: "The intendants of justice, and all other extraordinary commissions not verified in the Sovereign Courts, shall be immediately revoked."
Article 10 appears to do away with them altogether: "All extraordinary commissions shall remain revoked, all ordinances or
judgments rendered by the intendants of justice quashed and
annulled; the subjects of the King are prohibited from recognizing them as judges, or resorting to them, under penalty of a fine
of 10,000 livres. . . ." The King is thus deprived of one of the
two agencies through which he had exercised direct jurisdiction.

But he had used other means than robbing them of their jurisdictions to extend his authority at the expense of his officers:
he had forced them to do his will by various methods of coercion.
He could not dismiss them: they had an undisputed right to hold
their offices during good behavior, and the Courts were judges
of their behavior,[4] but there were other means of control than

---

[3] *Recueil de toutes les déclarations du roy* etc., 25-26; Isambert, XIV, 405.

[4] The irremovability of the officers of justice and finance is usually ascribed to
the venality of the offices: the officers had a property right in their offices. Documents of this controversy prove that irremovability was also constitutional; it was

the threat of dismissal. The Assembly attempted to provide against these. The King had reduced the officers' salaries; Article 4 states that no reductions in salaries shall be made except by edicts "well and duly verified" by the Courts with "liberty of suffrage." He had also created new offices, a danger to independence, not only because the new officers would be tools of the King, but also because the offices were venal, and an increase in number lessened their market value: the judges might be tempted to bend to the King's will rather than suffer in their estates. Article 19 forbade the establishment of new offices except by consent of the Courts. It is in part as follows: "In the future there shall be no creation of offices, either of judicature or finance, except by edicts verified in the Sovereign Courts with complete liberty of suffrage, for any cause, occasion, or under any pretext whatsoever, and the ancient constitution of the said sovereign companies cannot be changed or altered, either by increase in the number of officers or chambers, establishment of semesters, or by dismembering the jurisdictions of the said companies, in order to create and establish new ones." But the King's most effective arms against his officers had been interdiction and imprisonment. Defense against these is provided by Article 6: "No officer shall be troubled in the function and exercise of his charge by *lettres de cachet* containing prohibition to enter their companies, relegation to their houses, or to cities or castles of the kingdom, arrest or detention of their persons, or in any other manner than by informing against the officers and trying them according to the ordinances."

The King could not, then, deprive his officers of their jurisdictions, nor coerce them. He was also unable, according to the

founded upon an ordinance of Louis XI of the year 1467, in part as follows: "Nous, considerans qu'en nos officiers consiste, sous nostre authorité, la direction des faicts, par lesquels est policiée et entretenuë la chose publique de nostre Royaume, et que d'iceluy ils sont Ministres essentiaux, comme membres du Corps dont nous sommes le Chef, voulant extirper d'eux icelle doute, et pouvoir à la seureté en nostredit service, tellement qu'ils ayent cause d'y faire et perseverer ainsi qu'ils doivent; Statuons et ordonnons par ces presentes, que desormais nous ne donnerons aucuns de nos offices, s'il n'est vacant par mort, ou par resignation faite du bon gré et consentement du resignant, dont il apparoisse deüement, ou par forfaiture prealablement iugée et declarée iudiciairement, et selon les termes de Justice, par Juge competant." *Recueil de toutes les déclarations du roy*, etc., 26-27.

opposition, to alter the content of these jurisdictions by his command. By this I mean what follows.

The Courts claimed the right to sanction all royal acts affecting their jurisdictions; the word used was *verify*. It was a rule of the constitution that the King's edicts and ordinances were not valid until registered and published in the Sovereign Court or Courts in whose jurisdiction the matter of the act fell. The Court examined the act, and decreed registration if it was found satisfactory; if not, registration was refused, or, sometimes, the act was "modified," that is, ordered registered with amendments. But this rule was not always observed. The Sovereign Courts' right of verification was a serious limitation upon the power of the King, and there had been established a practice by which this limitation could be overcome. This was the *lit de justice*.[5] The King occupied his place in the Court[6] and had the act verified in his presence. The votes of the judges were taken, but only as a matter of form: it was held that in the King's presence they could not disagree with the King. The Courts denied the legality of this practice. This is the meaning of the phrase "with liberty of suffrage" which occurs in Articles 4 and 19, quoted above.

The *lit de justice* was one of the chief issues of the controversy, and deserves careful consideration. It will be remembered that the Fronde began with the opposition of the Parlement to the fiscal edicts registered at the *lit de justice* of January 15th, 1648. In the course of the dispute the constitutional question was thoroughly debated.

It was broached at the beginning, in the King's presence, by the Advocate General. The passage in his speech dealing with this subject, which was abridged at the beginning of Chapter I, is as follows.

"Sire, the *séance* of our Kings in their *lit de justice* has always been an action of ceremony, splendor, and majesty: all there is

---

[5] *Lettres de jussion*, a less extreme measure, do not figure in the controversy.

[6] During the Fronde, when the King came to the Parlement, the government frequently sent the Princes to the Chambre des Comptes and the Cour des Aides, where their presence had the same effect as that of the King in the Parlement.

of great and august in the kingdom appears on these occasions, when the visible and veritable signs of the royalty meet. Formerly the Kings your predecessors, on such days, caused to be heard by their peoples the great affairs of their State, the deliberations on peace or war, concerning which they asked advice of their Parlements and made reply to their allies: these actions were not then considered, as they are at present, as the effects of sovereign power, which spreads terror everywhere, but rather as assemblies of deliberation and counsel.

"The most ancient *lit de justice* held by our Kings is that of Charles V, in the year 1369, when he had the case of Edward Prince of Wales, his vassal, concerning the Duchy of Guyenne, tried in his presence. We could report to Your Majesty everything that happened during two centuries on such occasions, all of which were employed in the discussion of the great affairs of the State, such as the trials of great vassals of the Crown, the Dukes of Brittany, Bourbon, and Orleans, a King of Navarre, the Emperor Charles V in his quality of Count of Flanders; at other times to demand counsel on the execution of treaties of peace, to explain to the Parlement the motives of a war which the King desired to undertake, to announce the establishment of a Lieutenancy General to command during the absence of the King, in all of which circumstances the function of the officers of your Parlement was never diminished: the presence of our Kings did not close their mouths, and it was not thought of to use sovereign power as is done at present until the year 1563, when the pretext of religion, the refusal of the ecclesiastics to contribute to a holy war, made for this time the novelty tolerable. It is strange, then, that a thing done once without precedent, something which we could show to be contrary to its origin, now passes as ordinary usage, principally in the last twenty-five years, when in all public affairs, in the feigned or true necessities of the State, this course has been pursued! And in fact Francis I, a major King of thirty years, having complained in this place of the difficulties made in registering certain edicts which ordered the creation of new offices, did not cause the letters to be published in his presence, because he knew well that verification consists in liberty of suffrage, and that it is a kind of illusion in morals and a contradiction in politics to believe that edicts, which by the laws of the kingdom are not susceptible of execution until they have been brought to the Sovereign Companies and there debated, shall pass for verified when Your Majesty has had them read and published in his presence. And so all who have occupied our places, those great personages who have preceded us, whose memory will be always honorable because they defended courageously the rights of the King their master and the interests of the public, which are inseparable, have on like occasions cried out with much more vigor than we could possibly do; the Parlement has made remonstrances full of affection and fidelity, but without dissimulation, without complaisance or flattery.

"You are, Sire, our sovereign lord; the power of Your Majesty comes from above, who owe an account of your actions, after God, only to your conscience; but it concerns your glory that we be free men and not slaves; the grandeur of your State and the dignity of your Crown are measured by the quality of those who obey you."[7]

The Advocate General's doctrine, as it appears in this passage, may perhaps be summarized as follows: the *lit de justice* is unconstitutional; the King in resorting to it in the present circumstances is exceeding his just authority. Opposition, however, must be confined to remonstrances.

The Parlement, we saw, was less moderate than the Advocate General. On February 15th they ordered modification of one of the edicts registered at the *lit de justice.* The government immediately acted, and demanded an answer to a question which was a clear statement of the issue: "Did the Parlement pretend to modify an edict which had been verified with the King sitting in his *lit de justice?*" The Parlement finally yielded, but not, it would seem, entirely. They added the clause *sous le bon plaisir du roi* to their decree modifying the edict. This was to go farther than remonstrances.

---

[7] Talon, *Mémoires*, 209-210.

The Court held out for two weeks. During this time the constitutional question was thoroughly debated. Some of the arguments have been preserved in an anonymous manuscript journal of the Parlement, now in the *Archives Nationales*.[8] The absolutistic thesis was defended by the First President, Molé, and by President de Mesmes. The former distinguished as follows between ordinary royal acts and those registered at a *lit de justice:* "While in the other Edicts which are brought into the Court by the Procureur Général and are there deliberated on, we can proceed to verification with modifications, the Court contents itself on this so important occasion with Remonstrances or Supplications and is satisfied to attempt by these to obtain what it esteems should be changed."[9] President de Mesmes, implying that the Court's function was merely to enlighten the King as to the consequences of his acts, asserted that an edict registered at a *lit de justice* was an "authentic declaration of the will of the Prince" and as such should be obeyed. "The authority of our Kings," he said, "is in no way shared with their subjects; it resides quite entirely in their persons, without being communicated to their subjects."[10]

Among the champions of the authority of the Court was Le Coigneux. One of his speeches is reported as follows: "M. Le Coigneux showed that there were in our Kings two qualities, one of man, the other of King, which were so connected that without prejudice to the latter our Kings had found it good that their actions should ordinarily be examined in the Parlement; that this was done with great Justice, since the Court being established by the Kings to authorize all the contracts made in the Kingdom, their Edicts and Declarations are part of them, in which formerly the consent of the peoples was necessary, and now that of the officers of Justice, to whom has been given this power of consenting to the raising of impositions, as those who with greatest ability and reason know how to take care of the glory of the Prince and the necessity of the poor people; that

---

[8] *Debats du Parlement*, etc., No. U. 336.
[9] U. 336, 24.
[10] U. 336, 35.

nevertheless this law, authorized by the consent of all our Kings, did not prevent them from using sometimes their absolute power, when obliged to by present necessity, provided they have the approbation of their subjects in these circumstances, but that they should not use it except as a last resort, as did Charles IX in the year 1563, for the alienation of the property of the Church, and Henry IV, who in the whole course of his reign made use only once of this Royal authority, and then with great displeasure and in a very troublesome conjuncture of affairs. . . . Parlement had made no difficulty in declaring the Kings majors at the age of fourteen, because the state had nothing to fear from its Prince, whose actions and will are authorized by the consent of the peoples only as they are advantageous for their conservation."[11]

Le Coigneux admits the *lit de justice* in very exceptional circumstances, and by tacit popular consent. The passage is also interesting for the theory of the Parlement's authority, one which we shall see was held by many of the apologists of the opposition.

Another of the defenders of the Parlement, Le Cocq de Corbeville, asserted that there had been instances of the suspension of edicts registered at a *lit de justice* under a major King; that modification was permissible under a King who was a minor. His words were: "There is no reason for astonishment that there has been no example of the modification of an Edict brought by the King, since the case has never occurred of a minor King bringing an Edict to the Parlement, although on several occasions remonstrances have been made against edicts brought by major Kings with this clause: *and in the meantime it is forbidden to execute them;* that this could be shown to have happened in the reign of Charles IX, and principally under Louis XIII, notably in the verification of the ordinances of M. de Marillac, and in the edict of creation of the *Controlleurs des Productions des Procureurs.*"

Broussel, the great radical leader of the Parlement, affirmed the right of the Court to sanction all royal acts without exception. "The Parlement," he said, "should never appear in this opposition (to the King) except when the actions of the King were

[11] U. 336, 26-27.

contrary to the good of the State, and the Commands of God, not only as containing in themselves clauses prejudicial to the State, but for having been brought against the forms and the orders of the Company, which should always possess liberty of suffrage."[12]

The Parlement, we saw, after half yielding on the summons of the government, almost immediately modified another of the edicts. Then, under pressure, they again submitted. A few months later, however, when the Regent's authority had been ruined by the victory of the Courts, they made good their claim. It will be remembered that on August 19th the Parlement ordered that their decree of July 20th in regard to the Paris tariff should be substituted for one of the clauses of the edict registered at the *lit de justice* of July 31st. The next day President de Mesmes and the Duke of Orleans protested, but without success; the President was hooted down. The *Journal du Parlement* has the following description of this incident: "M. the President de Mesmes added that he esteemed it proper to add to the decree of the preceding day *sous le bon plaisir du Roy:* at this he was interrupted. He continued and said that if he were advancing his own personal opinion he would not object to being corrected with the civility which these gentlemen owed one another, and not tumultuously, but that he did not know how it was possible to reject his proposition, since it was in conformity with the Decrees of the Company, and notably with one of the month of January last, by which the Court had declared that the modifications which they had made and which they might make hereafter to Edicts verified the King sitting in Parlement, were only under his good pleasure. At this several began hooting to such a point that he was forced to stop speaking. After this M. the Duke of Orleans spoke and insisted that *sous le bon plaisir du Roy* be added, which was refused him."[13] The barricades came a few days after this session of the Parlement, and a new defeat of the government. The decree of August 19th was allowed to stand.

The Sovereign Courts, then, pretended to independent au-

---

[12] U. 336, 31.
[13] *Journal du Parlement*, at the date August 20, 1648.

thority in their jurisdictions. They could not be deprived of them, they could not be coerced, the content of their authority could not be modified without their consent.

It appears, further, that they considered themselves empowered to regulate by decree matters which lay within their competence, without the King's consent, and even against his expressed will. It will be remembered that the resolutions of the Assembly of the Chambre St. Louis were reported to the Parlement and there enacted. When the government intervened, they were grudgingly allowed to participate in the reform, but on condition that the royal acts embodying it should be in conformity with the will of the Courts. The Parlement debated two days before consenting to suspend execution of their first decrees, and then did it for a limited time, and *tacito senatusconsulto*. When the royal edicts which ordered these reforms were brought to the Parlement, they were found unsatisfactory, rejected, and finally altered by the government as the Court desired.

The Parlement debated their authority in this matter before taking action on the resolutions of the Assembly. Some of the arguments are given in the manuscript journal quoted above. The issue was whether the Court should proceed by remonstrance or by decree. The First President urged remonstrances: "M. the First President begged the Company to consider that everyone was in agreement in regard to the revocation of the Intendancies, and that there was diversity in opinion only on the means to obtain it, which he himself esteemed should be expected from the kindness of the Queen, in view of the danger of exciting her indignation if she were refused this mark of civility and honor, which she might desire; that one could depend, furthermore, upon her Justice and kindness, that she would give entire satisfaction to the just remonstrances of the Company."[14]

Broussel divided the recommendations of the Assembly into two classes, one coming under the authority of the King, the other under that of the Court, and urged action by Parlementary decree on the latter. His speech is reported as follows: "M. de Broussel . . . showed that in the different propositions which

[14] U. 336, 244-245.

would be made in the Chambre de St. Louis there were two kinds, some regarding the sole ministry of the royal authority, and the others which were enclosed within the district of the jurisdiction of the Company; that for the former it was necessary to implore by remonstrances the assistance of the royal authority, as for example the remission of verified tailles and subsidies, but that the others, being connected with the duty of our charges, we were obligated in conscience to legislate (*statuer*) upon them to put an end to the disorder of the kingdom by the legitimate means which the King has placed in the hands of his officers and of his Justice, and therefore he was of the opinion that the public should immediately experience the fruit of the deliberations of the Parlement, by forbidding all persons to accept any extraordinary commissions unless they are verified in the Court, to trouble the Treasurers of France, *Élus,* and other officers in the function of their charges; that commissions should be delivered to the Procureur Général of the King to inform against those who have in any manner stolen and diverted the finances of the King."[15]

The result of this discussion was, we have seen, that the Parlement decided to act by decree. According to the manuscript journal, this decision was made by a majority of forty: "The opinions being reduced to these two terms, either remonstrances alone, or immediate prohibition (*deffenses presentes*) to execute any extraordinary commissions not well and duly verified, with permission to inform against the malversations of those who have exercised them in the past, the last opinion prevailed . . . by forty voices, the first opinion being followed by 66 votes and the second by 106."[16]

It would appear, then, that the Courts came close to pretending to absolute authority in their spheres. According to them, public authority in France was divided: the King had his jurisdiction, and the Courts theirs. In certain matters, they seem to have held that the authority of the King and the Courts was coördinate. Among these was taxation. Their right to sanction

[15] U. 336, 234.
[16] U. 336, 245.

tax edicts is clearly affirmed in the third of the twenty-seven articles. It begins: "No impositions or taxes shall be levied except by virtue of edicts and declarations well and duly verified in the Sovereign Courts to whom cognizance of these matters belongs, with liberty of suffrage . . ." Their authority extended also to supervision of expenditure. By Article 8 of the Declaration of October 22nd, 1648, the King declared that in the future he would make use of *comptants* only for important and secret affairs of state.[17] The *comptants* were royal drafts on the treasury which were not passed on by the royal officers. The Chambre des Comptes registered this article with the following amendment: "The said *comptants* shall total no more than 3,000,000 livres a year, and they cannot exceed this sum."[18]

Just what the King's share of the state was, in the doctrine of the opposition, cannot be determined from the official documents. He had an appellate jurisdiction from the Sovereign Courts; Broussel gives him the right to remit taxes. There were also, of course, many other powers not mentioned in the documents of the controversy, but which no one would have denied him, such as provision of royal officers, and direction of foreign affairs and the military establishment.

The King's function is usually referred to vaguely as "the government." But even the government was not held to be beyond the reach of the Parlement. It will be remembered that the Court intervened in the controversy with the Parlement and city of Bordeaux. It appears further that they claimed a share in the direction of foreign affairs. Article 20 of the Treaty of Rueil reads: "When His Majesty sends deputies to treat with Spain for peace, he will willingly select some one of the officers of the Parlement of Paris to be present at the said treaty, with the same power as that given the others."[19]

Of the Courts, only the Parlement, it should be noticed, claimed these powers in government. The events as described in the first two chapters show clearly that the Parlement was

---

[17] Talon, *Mémoires*, 295.
[18] Talon, *Mémoires*, 310.
[19] Isambert, XVII, 163.

considered to occupy a position superior to the other Sovereign Courts. It was considered also to be superior to the provincial parlements. The *Journal du Parlement* mentions at the date February 27th, 1651 an eloquent speech of the First President "on the excellence of the Parlement of Paris, and the preëminence which it has over all the other Parlements."[20]

In his sphere of government, then, the King was subject to the counsel of the Parlement. It was held, further, that he must govern by the counsel of the Princes of the Blood.

Their authority was the chief issue in the second phase of the Fronde. The Parlement based their defense of the imprisoned Princes on the ground that they were members of the government. Molé spoke of them as follows to the Regent when delivering the Court's remonstrances for their release on January 20th, 1651: "The Princes of the Blood . . . are from the cradle Counsellors born of this Company . . . children of the House, the firmest stays of this Monarchy, and the most noble and most honorable members of this State."[21] When Condé broke with the Regent in July, 1651, Molé, speaking for the Court, urged her to make peace with him, since "the Princes of the Blood are as columns which should support the Crown, which being shaken, the State is in danger and threatened with ruin."[22]

The Princes claimed the right to participate in all the King's important affairs. One of Condé's complaints against the Regent in the summer of 1651 was that she had made appointments to the Council "without his participation and consent."[23] In his letter to the Duke of Orleans of September 13th, 1651, he says that the Queen's changing the Council without their consent was without reason or precedent "since of law the Princes of

[20] *Journal du Parlement*, at that date.

Some held that the Parlement was above the Estates General. President de Mesmes said in the Court on March 1st, 1649 "that the Parlements never went to these convocations of Estates since they were below them; but only that what was determined there was sent to them to be verified with the modifications which they judged necessary." *Journal du Parlement*, at the date March 1, 1649.

[21] *Journal du Parlement*, at the date January 20, 1651.

[22] *Journal du Parlement*, at the date July 18, 1651.

[23] *Journal du Parlement*, at the date August 17, 1651.

the Blood are Counsellors born of the State."[24] The Duke of Orleans in his letter to the King of August 9th, 1652 makes this right a matter of fundamental law: "The members of the King's Council are well instructed," he says, "in the fundamental laws of your State and of all the things that have happened since the establishment of this Monarchy; they are not ignorant of what share in your counsels belongs to those who have the honor to hold there my rank and that of my Cousin, especially during the state in which Your Majesty still is."[25]

The strongest statement I have found of this principle is in the speech of Bignon, Advocate General, on July 26th, 1652. Speaking of the award of the Lieutenancy General to the Duke of Orleans, he said that "the Court had not given the quality of Lieutenant General of the King to M. the Duke of Orleans, but had begged him to take it: in which he noticed that the Court had acted with their ordinary prudence, having begged the Duke of Orleans to take a quality which was due him by his birth, and by that the Court had shown that they did not mean to give a new or extraordinary quality to M. the Duke of Orleans, but only to indicate to him that he could take it of himself in necessary circumstances, since nature and blood gave it to him of full right; that this called to his mind a fine remark of King Henry IV who, being urged in the confusion of the disorders to take part in the government of the State under Henry III, though the latter was a Prince advanced in years, and who had given proof of great ability, replied that he would do it very willingly, not only as first Prince of the Blood, but also as first Magistrate of the Kingdom, which was a remark which gave proof of the kindness of his spirit, and showed a very special knowledge of these matters; and that the quality of Lieutenant General of the King offered to M. the Duke of Orleans was not new, that it was only a continuation of that which had been given to him by the King himself during his minority, which had, indeed, received some interruption of its action by the arrival of the civil majority of the King, but could nevertheless revive in necessary circum-

---

[24] *Journal du Parlement,* at the date September 13, 1651.
[25] *Journal du Parlement,* at the date August 9, 1652.

stances in his majority; that the present occasion was of those
which might move the kindness of M. the Duke of Orleans to
employ the rights of his birth for the good of the State."[26]

This speech was made after the massacre of the Hôtel de Ville,
and the speaker and the Court were in the power of the Princes.
Some months earlier, however, when the Court was free, they had
acknowledged an authority in the Duke almost equivalent to the
Lieutenancy General. It will be remembered that the decree of
December 29th, 1651, which put a price on Mazarin's head,
ordered the Duke of Orleans to employ "the King's authority
and his own" to enforce the declaration of the King and the
decrees of the Parlement against Mazarin.[27] This was after the
majority of the King.

It is evident from the events that the authority of the Princes
was not considered to be equal: Orleans was above Condé, and
Condé above Conti. When the Duke and the Prince were received at the Hôtel de Ville in April, 1652, the former was given
an armchair, the latter one without arms. Condé confessed the
superiority of the Duke of Orleans in a speech to the Parlement
on April 12th, 1652, reported as follows in the *Journal du Parlement:* "He begged the Company to be assured that he had never
had, and never would have, other intentions than to employ his
life for the service of the King and the good of the State, and to
follow entirely the orders of His Royal Highness and the sentiments of the Company, to which he always submitted with great
joy and satisfaction."[28] The explanation of this, as we shall see
later, is that the authority of the Princes varied with their
proximity to the throne.

It appears, then, that the opposition held that the King was
limited in his own sphere by the authority of the Princes of the
Blood, as well as by that of the Parlement. But this is not all.
They also maintained that the King could not delegate his authority, or, at least, that the power of delegation was confined
within certain limits. The attack on the minister, which was an

---

[26] *Journal du Parlement*, at the date July 26, 1652.
[27] Talon, *Mémoires*, 459-460.
[28] *Journal du Parlement*, at the date April 12, 1652.

issue in the first phase of the Fronde, and which was of prime importance in the second, was grounded on the illegality of the *ministériat*, or a limitation of it.

The strongest official statement on this subject is contained in the Parlementary remonstrances of January 21st, 1649. The Court there declared that when they had conferred the regency upon the Queen "they had been especially persuaded that, in order to maintain the legitimate liberty which causes Kings to reign in the heart of peoples, she would never allow an individual to rise to too great power to the prejudice of the sovereign, because she knew by the light which God gives to souls which he destines for the rule of states, how contrary such establishments are to the true rules of good order (*police*) in all sorts of governments, and especially in monarchies, which have for a fundamental law that there shall be only one minister in title and function; so that it is always shameful for the Prince, and injurious to his subjects that an individual should take too great a share of either his affections or his authority, since the former should be communicated to all, and the latter belongs to him alone. Furthermore (they go on to say) your Parlement had reason to believe that the personal experience of the Queen your mother would serve as a faithful guard against this evil, having seen during the time of her marriage, in the two notable examples of the Maréchal d'Ancre and Cardinal Richelieu, how monstrous is the elevation of a subject to too great favor and authority, and to what point dangerous and intolerable to his subjects."[29]

It is a fundamental law of monarchies that there should be only one minister in title and function. The King, then, must rule; he cannot delegate the exercise of his office. The reason for this is, that no one can have the same will to the good of the state as the King, to whom, and to whose successors, the chief position in the state belongs. A minister might sacrifice the interests of the state for his own profit; that the King should do so is unthinkable, since the state's evil is his own. This is implicit in another passage of this remonstrance: "As for the abuse of and depredations upon the finances, will Cardinal Mazarin

[29] Talon, *Mémoires*, 323-328.

dare say that there have been any limits to his covetousness? Sire, sovereigns, legitimate guardians of the people, consider their property as the property of another when they make use of it; and when they conserve it they look upon it as their own, so that they never lay hands on it except of necessity and with moderation. But the usurpers of sovereign authority consider the property of the people their prey; they are avid of their substance, and the last drop of their blood is the only limit of their cupidity."

This language is strong, but it is clear from other passages in the same document that the Parlement did not feel quite secure in this position. There they say that they have been forced to condemn the minister to justify their resistance to the King. "Your Parlement had a choice (after the blockade of Paris) between two courses, either to suffer the violence prepared, or to take arms for our common preservation. In one course or the other, it was necessary for your justification or for ours, to declare Cardinal Mazarin the enemy of Your Majesty and of the public, which prudence had caused us to postpone until then. If we were to perish, all the world should know that it was by the violence of our enemy, and not by that of our King, who never uses his force except to protect us; and if we were to defend ourselves, it should be equally notorious that it was against a tyrant, and not against our master, before whose name we prostrate ourselves, and for whom we have only sentiments of obedience."

In fact the Parlement never again went so far as to deny absolutely the legality of the *ministériat*. Subsequently the attacks upon the minister were founded upon the illegality of a foreigner's occupying a position in the Council, or upon the inviolability of the royal declaration against Mazarin.

There was precedent for the first contention in the Parlementary decree of 1617 against the Maréchal d'Ancre, which had forbidden entrance to the Council to foreigners. In 1651 this rule was extended to include naturalized foreigners (Mazarin had been naturalized) and, doubtless in memory of Richelieu, French cardinals: it will be remembered that this was the subject of the royal declaration registered on April 20th, 1651. An obvious justification of this rule was that it would protect the King against foreign influence, which might well be contrary to the interests of the state. Speaking of cardinals, Talon, in a speech to the Regent, said that their minds were divided between their obligations to the Pope and to the King, and cited the example of Cardinal Du Perron, who, at the Estates of 1614, had used his influence to prevent the adoption of an article declaring that the King had no superior in the temporal sphere. "Judge, madame," he said, "if those who feed upon and allow themselves to be poisoned by such propositions are fit for the ministry of the public affairs of the State."[30]

Whatever was the authority of the King in the doctrine of the opposition, it is evident that a Regent possessed much less. This appears from a number of official acts. The *maîtres des requêtes*, it will be remembered, founded their opposition to the edict of January 15th, 1648 on the ground that a Regent could not create certain offices. In the debates on the authority of the Parlement over edicts registered at a *lit de justice* one defense of the Court rested upon the inferiority of a Regent's power to that of the King.

The Regent being inferior to the King, during a regency a larger share of power devolves upon the other authorities of the state than normally. This appears in a passage of Molé's speech at the *lit de justice* of July 31st, 1648: "Your Majesty some day would reproach us justly, if, having been committed by you to employ all our vigils for the salvation of your people, we concealed the ills of the state, the oppression of the officers, the dissipation of the finances, the despair of the poor people."[31] The same principle is implicit in the phrase "especially during the state in which Your Majesty still is" at the end of the passage quoted from the Duke of Orleans' letter to the King of August 9th, 1652, and in a letter of Condé of September 13th, 1651: "History does not teach us," he says, "that at the age at which the King is at present, whatever abuse has been made of his

---

[30] Talon, *Mémoires*, 419-420.
[31] Isambert, XVII, 88.

authority, his Council has been closed to all the Princes of the Blood."[32]

Another consequence of this doctrine was that the commands of a Regent had less force than those of the King. The following passage is from the edict of amnesty of August 1652. Referring to the royal declaration which banished Mazarin, the King says: "Our said Court drew it up themselves and obliged us to publish it in their own terms, which we consented to, changing nothing, to avoid the tumults and the evils which we and our state were threatened with on the eve of our majority, the said declaration dated September last, and registered in the said Parlement the sixth of the same month. And these things are so public and so recent that they are known to everybody: after which it seemed that all pretexts of trouble and division should cease; and in addition with our majority, there was reason to hope that all our subjects would breathe only the obedience which is our due . . ."[33] In this last phrase the King implies that he is entitled to greater respect than the government of the minority. Further evidence of this principle is furnished by the course of events. Resistance was much firmer before the majority of the King than after. The most violent acts, it is true, occurred in the last year, but this violence seems desperate, rings false. The Fronde was principally a regency movement.

From what has gone before, it would seem that the constitutional theory of the opposition might be stated as follows: public authority in France is divided between the King, the Courts, and the Princes, and during a regency the Courts and the Princes possess a larger share of authority than normally.

The doctrine of the division of authority involves logically the right of resistance: an authority which is independent must defend itself against coercion. The events of the Fronde seem to indicate that this conclusion was accepted. When the city of Paris rose against the royal government to secure the release of Broussel, the Parlement refused to order the rebels to lay down their arms until the judges had returned. When the government

[32] *Journal du Parlement,* at the date September 13, 1651.
[33] Isambert, XVII, 290-291.

ordered the Court out of Paris in January 1649 and laid siege to the capital to enforce this command, the Parlement raised an army for their defense. The revolt of 1651 was to deliver the Princes from prison, and that of the following year mainly to defend them from the attempt to exclude them from the government.

These acts of the Parlement, however, were accompanied with explanations which indicate that even during a regency the Court were not quite certain of their right to resist by force the royal authority. Their refusal at the time of the barricades to comply with the request of the King's attorneys to order the people of Paris to lay down their arms was based not upon the right of resistance, but upon the plea that it would be impolitic to compromise their authority by giving orders which would not be obeyed. The First President said: "that in truth the conclusions were quite good, but that it was to be feared that the people would not disarm until they had seen M. de Broussel, whatever decree the Court might make, and that thus it was necessary to be very careful not to hazard their authority."[34] We have already seen in a passage quoted above from the remonstrances of January 21st, 1649 that the Parlement's resistance during the blockade of Paris was on the ground that they were opposing not the King but the Minister: "it was necessary for your justification or for ours to declare Cardinal Mazarin the enemy of Your Majesty and of the public . . . if we were to defend ourselves, it should be notorious . . . that it was against a tyrant, and not against our master, before whose name we prostrate ourselves, and for whom we have only sentiments of obedience."

The King is a master, before whose name the judges prostrate themselves: if the blockade of Paris had been ordered by the King, the Parlement could not have resisted. This is a confession of the obligation of absolute obedience, and as such contradicts the theory of independent authority which is that upon which they usually acted. But the Court is still far from a complete capitulation. The phrase "for your justification" is full of mean-

---

[34] *Journal du Parlement,* at the date August 28, 1648.

ing. The King is subject to justice; if he is alone in the government, he is bound to do right.[35]

2. DECLARATIONS OF THE GOVERNMENT

The character of the pronouncements of the government during the Fronde is variation: claims for the King change with the fortunes of the party; very high when they were victorious, they are much more moderate, close to the theory of the opposition, when in difficulties.

The preamble of the Declaration of July 31st, 1648, while denying the legality of the Assembly of the Chambre St. Louis, admits the right of the Sovereign Courts to sanction the acts of the King. It is, in part, as follows: "As there is nothing which does more to maintain and preserve monarchies in their perfection than the observance of good laws, it is the duty of a great prince to take care, for the welfare and the salvation of his subjects, lest they be corrupted by the abuses which creep unobserved into the most perfect states, so as to avoid the ruin which might occur, if by negligence the evils became so powerful that they should be unable to support the remedies. Therefore the Kings our predecessors, to prevent these accidents, which cause often the destruction of the most powerful monarchies, have from time to time convoked (*ordonné*) assemblies to discover and recognize the imperfections and disorders which have been formed in their states, and to advise the best means to remove them. And these assemblies, whether of estates[36] or notables,

[35] A second line of defense is indicated in another passage of this remonstrance: by natural law the people have the right to resist an unjust ruler. This stand was taken, we shall see (Chapter V, Section I), by some of the apologists of the opposition. The passage reads as follows: "Death, however terrible it may be, with its most horrible pomp and display, could not cause us as much fear as the least omission in observation of and submission to all that bears your (the King's) character; and although natural law, more ancient and more absolute than all the others, gives us all legitimate means to conserve what it has freely bestowed upon us, if we had judged this martyrdom innocent and not conducive to your ruin and inevitably, following that, to the ruin of your state, we would have preferred to die rather than to make use of the privilege of nature to defend ourselves against the armies commanded under the name of our sovereign." Talon, *Mémoires*, 327.

[36] Considerable power is given the Estates General in two of the government's pronouncements. The King's letter of April 4, 1651, to the *baillis*, convoking the

have always been convoked and regulated (*ordonnées et réglées*) by them, since by the law of the kingdom no body can be established to take cognizance of the government and administration of the monarchy except by the authority and power of the King; and so these assemblies, as they are summoned by the sovereigns, after they have recognized the abuses which it was necessary to correct, and when they have advised the best means to correct them, have always presented to the Kings the *cahiers* of their remonstrances to serve them as matter to make laws and ordinances as they judge best, which are then sent to the sovereign companies, established principally to authorize the justice of the acts (*voluntés*) of the King, and to cause them to be received by the people with the respect and veneration which is their due . . ."[37]

The Courts had been established principally to authorize the justice of the acts of the King. This was to admit the claims of the opposition almost in their entirety: the Courts have authority almost coördinate with that of the King.

When this declaration was made, however, the government was acting under the dictation of the Courts. Their real opinion must be looked for in pronouncements made in other circumstances.

In the royal declaration of July 31st, 1652, transferring the Parlement of Paris to Pontoise, the King gives a degree of authority to the judicial, financial, and even the military administrations, but subordinates them strictly to himself: "All author-

Estates General, begins by asserting that there was no better way to put a stop to the disorders than to assemble the Estates General, in order to apply remedies "on their complaints and supplications and by their good advice (*par leurs bons avis*)." Isambert, XVII, 241. The Estates produce matter out of which the King makes law. The King could take what he wanted, but from this language it would seem that he was bound to take something. The following passage is from a response of the King of February 26th, 1649: In case Spain continued to refuse the government's conditions for peace, the Regent "would consider herself under obligation to consult the opinion of the Estates General of the kingdom, which have already arrived, and will soon be assembled, on the decision to be made, there being no doubt that it would be the best, since it would have been made by the general consent of all the orders of the kingdom." Isambert, XVII, 135.

[37] Talon, *Mémoires*, 256-257.

ity," he says, "belongs to us. We hold it of God alone, and no person, of whatever quality he may be, can pretend to any part of it. . . . The functions of justice, of arms, of finance, should be always distinct and separate; the officers of the Parlement have no other power than that which we have deigned to entrust to them, to render justice to our subjects. They have no more right to regulate (*ordonner*) and take cognizance of what is not of their jurisdictions, than the officers of our armies and our finances would have to render justice, or establish presidents and counsellors to exercise it. . . . Will posterity ever believe that officers have presumed to preside over the general government of the Kingdom, form councils and collect taxes, to assume, finally, the plenitude of a power which belongs only to us?"[38]

The government here reserves for the King the "general government of the Kingdom," but allows the officers to "regulate and take cognizance" of matters which lie within their jurisdictions. A like distinction is implied in one of the declarations registered at the *lit de justice* of October 22nd, 1652. This reads in part: "We have forbidden and forbid the persons holding our so-called Court of Parlement of Paris hereafter to take cognizance of the general affairs of our State and the direction of our Finances, or to order or undertake anything for reason of these matters against those to whom we have entrusted the administration of them, under penalty of disobedience."[39]

Other declarations of the government were less moderate. The decree of the Council of June 15th, 1648, quashing that of the Parlement which ordered assemblies of the deputies of the Sovereign Courts, contains the following passage: "The said decree is an act of disobedience full of contempt and injurious to the royal authority, which cannot, without diminution, permit officers, who have no other authority than that which is given them by the Kings, to be exercised within the rules which are prescribed to them, to use that authority by a violent usurpation to resist the will of their King and their master."[40] The Court

[38] Isambert, XVII, 288-289.
[39] *Journal du Parlement*, at the date October 22, 1652.
[40] Talon, *Mémoires*, 236.

has, then, in its own right, no part of the state, no authority but that which the King chooses to give; the judges are merely the delegates of the King. This is implicit in the use of the present tense: authority which is given them, not has been given them, and in the word master. This theory appears more distinctly in the declaration of January 23rd, 1649, which suppressed the Parlement of Paris. It reads in part: "It is inconceivable blindness that magistrates instituted by the Sovereign to render justice to his subjects, who have no authority which is not formed by the hand of the Kings, who can consequently suspend it or withdraw it when they abuse it, should undertake to raise that authority above that of the Kings themselves, to lay hold of the government and the administration of the state by an act of usurpation for which there is no example in past ages. . . . Unable longer to suffer, without failing in what we owe ourselves, the assaults of a company which has no other legitimate power than that which we have given them . . . we have finally resolved . . . to extinguish and suppress entirely this Company, and to withdraw the power which they hold of us."[41]

It would appear from this evidence that the government hesitated between two views of the power of the officers: one, that though they had no authority in the "government," they had certain rights in their jurisdictions; the other, that they were the simple agents of the King.

The official declarations show that the government and the opposition held widely divergent views in regard to the organization of authority in the kingdom. They also indicate that the two constitutional theories rested upon different theoretical bases.

The argument of the opposition is legal; every one of their claims was justified by precedent, previous practice in the monarchy. When the Courts affirmed their right to independent jurisdictions, they alleged their authority, the Ordinance of Blois, and that of Louis XI; when they claimed the power to sanction the important acts of the King, they showed that they

[41] There is a copy of this declaration in pamphlet form in Widener Library: Fr. 1281.2.5, No. 9.

had been in possession of this power until recent times. The government used precedents at times, but not usually, and not as much as they might have, since the Courts probably went beyond their legal rights. In most of their pronouncements, as in the following, the law is referred to in a perfunctory manner: "How have they (the Parlement) the insolence to advance those fair and true political maxims, that Monarchies have for fundamental law, that there should be only one master in title and function, while they are attempting to sap its foundations? It is for the conservation of this so holy law that we are now armed against them; we want to maintain it, and they would like to destroy it by establishing a monstrous power, and making an authority of two hundred heads of our Monarchy (*un chef à deux cent têtes de nostre Monarchie*). We are not ignorant of those maxims, that the unity of power and authority is the soul of Monarchies, which leads them to their perfection; and that is the reason why the Kings our predecessors have so often restricted the Parlement of Paris within the limits of their function, and have not allowed them to encroach in the slightest degree upon the sovereign power, or to intervene in the affairs of state, foreseeing clearly that the consequences would be dangerous, as we see to-day. Those great and virtuous persons, who in other times filled their positions so worthily, were not ignorant of these maxims, and observed them religiously; that wise and faithful minister, First President de la Vaquerie, applied them well when he replied to the complaints which Louis XII proposed through his chancellor, before coming to the throne, that the Court of Parlement was not established to take cognizance of affairs of state."[42]

In this passage the government's case rests not upon the precedent cited, which is very weak, but upon a rational argument: the unity of power and authority is the soul of monarchies. A remark of Mazarin's shows that he was quite willing to date from recent times the form of the state to which he appealed. Speaking of the opposition in 1643, he said that they "would reduce matters to the state they were in when France, though

[42] Isambert, XVII, 151-152.

apparently governed by a King, was in reality a republic." He referred to the Kingdom as it had been before Louis XIII.[43] The Fronde, it appears, was not a legal controversy, a dispute over the interpretation of the law, but a conflict between law and "reason."

[43] This is from Lacour-Gayet, *L'Education Politique de Louis XIV*, 279. The passage reads: "Elle (la France) n'avait plus alors ces sentiments que Mazarin avait notés en 1643, quand elle travaillait à défaire ce qui avait été fait sous le règne de Louis XIII, pour l'établissement de l'autorité royale absolue et independante, quand elle voulait 'réduire les choses comme au temps où la France, bien qu'en apparence gouvernée par un roi, était en réalité une république.' "

CHAPTER IV

DEFENSE OF THE GOVERNMENT

THE official declarations show that the government and the opposition held different views in regard to the constitution of authority in the kingdom. They also indicate that behind this conflict over authority were opposed views in regard to the nature of the government. For further information we turn to the works written in defense of the parties, starting with the apologists of the government.

1. ABSOLUTISM

The works written in defense of the government are few and incomplete, and I shall supplement them with a book written some sixteen years before the Fronde, Le Bret's *De la Souveraineté du Roy*, the great apology of Richelieu's government. This seems permissible in consideration of the fact that Mazarin's policy was generally held to be modeled upon that of Richelieu; we shall see, further, that a number of government writers in the Fronde take positions close to those of Le Bret.

It will be remembered that the government in some of their declarations allowed a degree of authority to the royal officers, but subordinated them strictly to the King. This appears to be the opinion of Le Bret. "Cognizance of the rights of the King," he says, "belongs to his officers, according to the attribution which is made to them by the Edicts and Ordinances. In which should not be comprehended the things which concern the administration and the government of the State, the cognizance of which is reserved to the sole person of the King, and no one else has the power to meddle with these matters except by his order and his commission, according to the fundamental law of the monarchy, whereby the sovereign command (*commandement*) resides in a single person, and obedience in all the others."[1]

But Le Bret is thinking here of the officers of justice. His book contains little or nothing on the financial administration, and he refuses all independent authority to the military officers. Concerning the latter he says: "Although we have at present in France several military charges erected in title of perpetual office, such as Constable and Marshals of France: nevertheless it is certain that the King, according to circumstances, can commit the command of his armies to whomever he chooses."[2]

He hedges on the power of the officers of justice. Of evocations he says: "They are judged in the Privy Council of the King, because they can be made only by his Sovereign power, since they are a kind of privilege against the order of the Jurisdictions, which desires that everyone plead before his natural judge. I use this word, because veritably it is an order which has been established by nature herself."[3] There are only two just causes for evocation: denial of justice, and when the judge is related to a party. Nevertheless he insists upon the subordination of the Parlements to the King and his Council: "These Parlements," he says, "have under them the *Baillis* and the *Sénéschaux*, to keep them to their duties and correct them if they happen to fail in their judgments, and in all the rest of their charges: as also the Parlements have over them the King, assisted by his Chancellor, and by his Council of State, to receive their correction if in anything they go beyond the power which has been given them, or if they happen to do something contrary to the good of the service of his Majesty and to the welfare of the Kingdom."[4] He also insists upon the legality of special commissions: "I know that one can infer from the Edict of Blois, Article 98, that the King has tied his hands, and can no longer give such commissions, desiring that each matter be sent to the officers who should naturally have cognizance of it. But he intended to forbid them

---

[1] Le Bret, *De la Souveraineté du Roy*, in the section entitled *Choses obmises*.
[2] Le Bret, *De la Souveraineté du Roy*, 166.
[3] Le Bret, *De la Souveraineté du Roy*, 497.
[4] Le Bret, *De la Souveraineté du Roy*, 156-157.

only for private affairs, and which concern the interests of individuals; because on these occasions it is not reasonable to make any change in the order which has been established by usage and by the ordinances: and not when it is a question of public affairs, and which touch the State: the reason being, doubtless, that since he has reserved to himself the cognizance of these matters, according to the edict of Charles VIII, he can commit such persons as he pleases to have cognizance of them."[5]

The judicial authority of the courts, then, is strictly subject to royal control; as for legislative authority, we shall see in a moment that they have none. Nevertheless, according to Le Bret, the King's officers of justice have a limited authority. We shall see that he also gives a certain amount of power to the officers of the Church. But with these exceptions, and they are practically very slight, all constituted authority is in the King.

The Princes of the Blood and the Children of the Kings have no authority in the state. Though they possess the privilege of exemption from capital punishment, "nevertheless," Le Bret says, "they have no more authority in the State than the other subjects . . . still it is proper (*de la bien séance*) for the King, after having recognized their prudence and their good conduct, to give them employment, and to communicate to them their counsels."[6]

The Estates General have no independent authority: summons depends upon the King, and he is not obliged to follow their advice. But having deprived them of power, Le Bret champions them against those who would do away with them; this opinion, he says, is to be received in tyrannical and seignorial states, not in a royal state like France: "It is there (in the Estates) that are published the ordinances, which being similar to those ancient laws of the Romans called *centuriatae*, which the consuls proposed to the assembly of the whole city, are received and observed by the people with much more obedience and respect than those which are published at other times."[7]

[5] Le Bret, *De la Souveraineté du Roy*, 149-151.
[6] Le Bret, *De la Souveraineté du Roy*, 56-57.
[7] Le Bret, *De la Souveraineté du Roy*, 644.

The King, then, practically monopolizes public authority. This does not mean, however, that he is free to do as he chooses. Le Bret indicates at least six limitations upon the power of the King.

He is first of all under divine law. In Chapter VI, *On the Commands and Rescripts of the Sovereign Prince, and the Obedience which is due them*, he says "I will say in the first place that the most famous theologians and politicians teach that one owes no obedience to Kings, when they command something which is contrary to the command of God";[8] and later in the book: "the Precept of the Apostle . . . enjoins us expressly to obey the Prince, *tamquam praecellenti;* that is to say, without any exception: unless it be for things which contravene directly the commands of God."[9]

Chapter IV, *On the Fundamental Laws of the Sovereign Crown of France*, deals with the law of succession to the crown. "The kingdom," he says, "is conserved by successive right." Though he does not affirm it directly, this is, of course, a limitation upon the royal authority: it is beyond the power of the King to deprive his successor of the crown.

The King also, according to Le Bret, is bound to respect the rights of private property. In Chapter X, *In what Cases the Sovereign Prince can dispose of the goods of individuals against their will*, the opposed doctrine is condemned in unequivocal terms: "Some old (*anciens*) writers, by shameful and servile flattery, have put it forward that subjects possess their goods by precarious title and usufruct, and that property in them belongs to the King by right of sovereignty."[10] In public emergencies the King can take the goods of his subjects, but ordinarily he must pay for them, the only exception being accidents of war, such as destruction of crops.

Chapter VIII deals with the subject of the King's contracts and treaties. Le Bret here makes the rather surprising statement that the King is bound by promises which he has made to his

---

[8] Le Bret, *De la Souveraineté du Roy*, 188.
[9] Le Bret, *De la Souveraineté du Roy*, 512.
[10] Le Bret, *De la Souveraineté du Roy*, 632.

subjects in order to bring a rebellion to a close. The King is also incapable of contracting an alliance with an infidel state, and he can ally with a non-Catholic state only under certain circumstances: "And as for those who revere the same Redeemer as we, but who have different opinions in the Religion which he has taught us, I would have it considered whether they want to use our alliance to advance their religion and to weaken ours: for in this case there is no doubt that it would be impiety to join our arms with theirs. But if it is to aid one another in the common defense of our goods, lands, and Seignories, I think that one cannot object to such confederations."[11]

It is evident from the last passage that Le Bret is troubled by the Church; this is, in fact, one of his chief preoccupations: he whittles down ecclesiastical authority as much as he can, but when he is through, something still remains as a barrier to the authority of the King. The Church legislates in faith and doctrine: "Since the guardianship and the protection of the Church is committed to the Kings, and since by their oath they obligate themselves to defend it and conserve it with all their power, there is no doubt that for what touches that protection, they may make laws in Ecclesiastical matters: *not to define anything of faith or doctrine, nor to examine the holy decrees of the Church,* but to authorize them and enforce their execution."[12] Further, the King has no jurisdiction over bishops, though Le Bret would put this not upon the law, but upon the piety of the King.[13]

The last of the limitations upon the royal power which I find in Le Bret is the denial of the validity of *lettres de cachet.* Obedience is due from judges only "to letters patent, *signées en commandemens,* and sealed with the great seal . . . which may serve as legitimate evidence of the will of the Prince."[14] It is evident in the last phrase that Le Bret did not consider this a final limi-

---

[11] Le Bret, *De la Souveraineté du Roy,* 618.

[12] My italics. Le Bret, *De la Souveraineté du Roy,* 76.

[13] Le Bret, *De la Souveraineté du Roy,* 93.

[14] Le Bret, *De la Souveraineté du Roy,* 201.

I recall one more limitation: he says in Chapter X that changes in the coinage should be made only by the "advis et par une commune deliberation de tous les Ordres."

DEFENSE OF THE GOVERNMENT

tation. In fact, as is well known, the seals were entirely at the disposal of the King: he could at any time take them from the keeper and give them to another person.

Within these limits the King is free. In legislation he is not bound by the ordinances or the customs of the kingdom. "There is no doubt," Le Bret says, "that the Kings may use of their power and change the ancient laws and ordinances of their states. Which is to be understood not only of the general laws, but also of the municipal laws and the individual customs of the provinces: for they may change them too, when necessity and justice demand it. . . . But it is asked: if the King can make all these changes of laws and ordinances of his own authority, without communicating them to his sovereign courts. To which is replied that there is no doubt of it, because the King is the only sovereign in his kingdom, and sovereignty is no more divisible than the point in geometry. Nevertheless it will always be good form (*bien séant*) for a great King to have his Laws and Edicts approved by his Parlements, and his other principal Officers of the Crown. . . . Thus we see by our annals that this custom was observed anciently among us."[15]

The King also possesses the taxing power. Le Bret makes a great point of this; it is, he says, the distinguishing mark of absolute monarchy: "Aristotle says, that there are two kinds of monarchies: one absolute, and the other whose power is limited. . . . The first could of their sole authority, and without the consent of their subjects, impose Tailles, and raise subsidies, when they judged it necessary for the good of their affairs. But these last did not have this power, except by the consent of their peoples, and for urgent and reasonable causes. And although the kingdom of France has always been fully monarchical . . . nevertheless our ancient Kings governed themselves at the beginning with such moderation, that they raised very little from their subjects, because the revenues of their Crown were then sufficient to support their expense. But since war, like a devouring fire has consumed most of their domain, they have been obliged to use their authority absolutely, and to raise from their

15 Le Bret, *De la Souveraineté du Roy*, 69-72.

people Tailles and subsidies; even without their consent: which
is one of the most remarkable rights of the Sovereignty of the
Kings, and which is so peculiar to them that it has always been
held a maxim that there are none but they who have the power in
their Kingdoms to raise impositions from the peoples of their
obedience."[16] No privilege can stand against the King's right
to tax: Le Bret approves of a law mentioned by Livy whereby
in time of war "all privileges and all immunities ceased, so that
all contributed to the relief of one another, in common misery."[17]
The property of the Church is not legally exempt: "And though
it can be maintained that our Kings, being protectors and
founders of churches, can of full right raise impositions from
Ecclesiastics: nevertheless they have been so religious that they
have never done it except by consent of the Pope, and of all the
Clergy; and for causes so just and legitimate that they could not
decently be refused."[18]

The King of France, then, according to Le Bret, practically
monopolizes public authority in the kingdom. That authority
is very extensive, including the power to tax, and the power to
make and to change the civil law. It is not, however, unlimited;
the King is bound to respect private property; he cannot violate
a treaty with his subjects; he cannot ally with an infidel; he cannot compel the judges to obey a *lettre de cachet;* he cannot deprive
his successor of the crown; he cannot issue a command in violation of divine law.

The King, though possessing great power, is nevertheless limited. But suppose he goes beyond that power, violates these
limitations: is there any remedy? Le Bret struggles with this
problem. The chapter on treason he considers the high point of
his book: "And since the occasion is presented to speak of such
an atrocious crime, I should consider that I had not given my
courage its entire perfection, if I did not show in this place, in
what consists the enormity of such a wicked act, and what pen-
alties it merits for its punishment."[19] A person is guilty of high

[16] Le Bret, *De la Souveraineté du Roy*, 395-396.
[17] Le Bret, *De la Souveraineté du Roy*, 418.
[18] Le Bret, *De la Souveraineté du Roy*, 111-112.
[19] Le Bret, *De la Souveraineté du Roy*, 527-528.

treason who entertains the intention of killing the Prince, consults an astrologer on the length of his life, or even speaks ill of his actions. But in another place Le Bret says there is one case in which the King can be disobeyed, and implies that he may be resisted: that is when he is guilty of violating divine law. I have already quoted this passage in part; I give it here at greater length: "It should be held as a maxim that although the Sovereign Prince goes beyond the just measure of his power, it is not for that reason permissible to resist him." Those who say that the people cannot, but that the officers and magistrates can, are wrong: "It would overturn the whole order of the Monarchy, if it were permitted Officers to resist the Ordinances of the Prince; it would make them his equals, even his superiors: it would be to go against the Precept of the Apostle, who enjoins us expressly to obey the Prince, *tamquam praecellenti;* that is to say, without any exception: unless it be for things which contravene directly the commands of God."[20]

So much for the doctrine of the outstanding apologist of the preceding administration. During the Fronde, the main questions treated by the defenders of the government were the authority of the Parlement, the legal limitations upon the King's authority, and the right of resistance. To all of these, answers were made which are close to those of Le Bret; there was a tendency, however, to take a more advanced stand.

Le Bret gave an undefined authority to the officers of justice. A like position is taken in several of the works in defense of the government. A pamphlet[21] distributed in Paris during the blockade by an agent of the government, while denying that the Parlement has power in "government," gives the Court authority in the administration of justice. The passage is as follows: "In what place in their registers will the Parlement find that they can prescribe to the King the choice of his ministers? What laws of the Kingdom or what usage gives them authority to dismiss them when they are not agreeable to them? What right has the Parlement, being instituted only to render justice to private per-

---

[20] Le Bret, *De la Souveraineté du Roy,* 527-528.
[21] *Le roi veut que le Parlement sorte de Paris,* etc.

sons, to put their hand on the government of the State? Are we in some Republic? And is the King no more than our Doge?" The same doctrine is set forth in the *Request of the Peoples of France*,[22] which says: "Just as a brook would dry itself up if it exhausted the spring which gives it birth, so your authority would finally be lost, and would infallibly destroy itself, if it undertook to ruin that of the King, from whom it derives its virtue (*tire son principe*); if the Kings have done you the honor to make you feel the brilliance of their purple (*de vous ressentir de l'éclat de leur pourpre*), they have never had the intention of robbing themselves of it; and if it has pleased them to leave with you quite a considerable part of their authority, they have never intended to share with you the Majesty of the Empire, which resides originally and incommunicably in their sacred person." This authority which the King has left with the Parlement is limited to judicial administration and remonstrances: "All the authority which is contained in these two names (Court and Parlement) is restricted to judgments in matters of dispute between subjects (*Arrests pour la Iustice contentieuse*) and Remonstrances against the Edicts of the Sovereign; no more can be pretended to without usurpation."

Other government apologists take the stand which we saw assumed in certain official declarations, that the judges are merely the delegates of the King. One passage in the *Sentiments of a Faithful Subject of the King*[23] reads: "Reason and all sorts of duties order us to prefer incomparably the will of the King to the will of a Parlement which can have no just will but that of the King"; and another: "The Magistrates hold in homage from the Prince all the rights which they have to command the people, and to render justice." This idea is stated more explicitly in a passage in the *Blindfold removed from the Eyes of the Parisians*.[24] It reads: "And I see no reason why the Parlement of Paris, which is only one of the nine Parlements of France, to all of which only distributive justice in their jurisdictions, between per-

[22] *Requeste des peuples de France*, etc.
[23] *Les sentimens d'un fidelle suiet du Roy*, etc.
[24] *Le Bandeau levé de dessus les yeux des Parisiens*, etc.

sons in those jurisdictions, has been entrusted by the King and
his predecessors, can take to themselves the right to control
(*syndiquer*) the actions of the King and the Queen Regent, his
mother, any more than the eight other Parlements and a larger
number of Companies as Sovereign as theirs, and which have in
truth the same power from the King to judge differences between
all private persons, but only *so long as it shall please his Majesty*,
as they will see in their letters."

Le Bret declared that the King was above the civil law. This
is also asserted in the best government pamphlet I have read,
the *Christian and Political Answer to the Erroneous Opinions of
the Time.*[25] To the proposition *That the King is Subject to the
Laws* this writer replies: "The law is an ordinance of the Sovereign, who alone can make them, for who has greater interest in
watching over the members than he who is the head; it is, then,
the work of the King, and just as the workman is above his work,
so one cannot deny that the Kings are above their laws, as the
father is above the son, and the master above the servant. Saint
Jerome says that one should not seek the reason of the law but
the authority, and Saint James: if you judge the law, you are
not observer but judge . . . and just as what is not commanded
by the Law of God and of the Church is indifferent, it is done
justly because the King has ordered it, or unjustly because he
has forbidden it; for as for the temporal laws, nothing is just of
itself, but takes the form of justice or injustice according as it
pleases the King to command, and because he commands it, it
must be observed; if one contravenes his command, one does
evil, since he transgresses what is commanded by the Superior,
who can punish the transgressor. . . . Since laws are made by
Kings, they are not obligated by them: for no one is constrained
by himself, *Princeps liber est, sutque ac legem potens.* Seneca too
says, *Legis auctorem, lege non teneri.* There is no doubt that the
King can dispense from the Laws, moderate them or augment
them as he judges best for the good of his State. . . . All seditious rebels always cover themselves with this cloak, and say
that the laws and ordinances of the Kingdom have been violated,

[25] *Response chrestienne et politique*, etc.

as if it were not only permissible to Kings, but necessary to violate them, to bend them, or to hold them rigid, according as they see it proper and more useful for the public good and the interests of their State. It is a seditious opinion to believe that he who has the sovereign power is subject to the civil laws, the state not being able to obligate itself, either to itself or to any individual. The Prince or the Senate compose the State, whose being subsists only in the exercise of the sovereign power."

From the phrase "what is not commanded by the law of God and of the Church is indifferent" one would conclude that this writer considered that the King was bound only by the positive commands of Scripture and the Church. In another passage of this pamphlet, however, the King is subject to justice. I quote at length, for reasons which will be apparent later. "It is true that the King is obliged, and promises at his Consecration, to render Justice, and to govern his Kingdom according to right and reason; when he does not keep his promise God, who is sole Judge of his actions, will not leave his injustice unpunished, but it does not belong to subjects to take cognizance of them, nor to judge if his commands are just and reasonable, for if it were permissible, everyone would be King above the King, since he would have power not only to control what he did, but also to take all that seemed to him reasonable, and to reject everything that he did not approve. The Kings, to show their sovereign power, and that they are obliged to render an account of their actions to God alone, use these words *Car tel est nostre plaisir*, as the Sovereign Courts say in their decrees, And for cause without giving cause, to show their sovereignty. I admit that formerly the Kings did not speak in this way, nor with an authority as absolute as they have done in the last few centuries, nevertheless it is crime of high treason, and a very pernicious and wicked thing to desire to reëstablish what was anciently observed . . . those who want to speak of the power of the ancient Kings of France, and of their way of acting, to draw consequences for the present time, would be guilty of putting forward seditious and pernicious propositions, as if it were said that the King ought to share France and divide it into four Kingdoms, because Clovis the first Christian King, did it, and several Kings after him."

The King, then, must govern justly and reasonably. But what does this mean? The usual answer is that of Le Bret: the King must respect property rights. In the *Reply and Refutation of the Lettre d'Avis*[26] the government of the Grand Turk is condemned because he has power over the lives and goods of his subjects; this is tyranny, and contrary to God's establishment.

The defenders of the government devote themselves mainly to the problem of resistance. Le Bret, we have seen, allowed resistance to a command in violation of divine law. I have found no government writer of the controversy who in any case allows a right of resistance. There are some, however, who admit disobedience.

Resistance is prohibited in all cases in the *Blindfold Removed from the Eyes of the Parisians*.[27] The passage reads: "And so the Majesty of our Kings is the image of the Divine: he who attacks one, attacks the other. And just as there is no just cause for blaspheming God, so there is none to attack the Sovereign power by Him established: if the smallest opening is permitted, the Royalty ceases to be, and remains in dispute between them who were Subjects and him who was King, but are no longer one or the other. . . . There are no remonstrances, however humble they may feign to be, which, when obedience has ceased, are not rebellions, hardly dissimilar to the reverences which the Jews made to the Savior of the world when they crucified Him. Prayers are indeed permitted us; but if they are not found just, it is impiety toward Heaven, it is a crime against the King, to mutiny against him and attempt, like the giant of the Metamorphoses, to use force to obtain obedience from him who should command. No subject, Philip of Comines says it, has ever profited from attempting even to frighten his master."

Though condemning resistance, it is evident from another passage in the pamphlet that this author would allow disobedience in certain cases. The passage is as follows: "We have been obliged, you say, to take arms by necessity, mistress of the Laws.

[26] *Responce et refutation du discours intitulé Lettre d'Avis*, etc.
[27] *Le Bandeau levé de dessus les yeux des Parisiens*, etc.

Those who treat of *cas de conscience* are not agreed that there is any just cause for raising arms against one's Prince, any more than for being a parricide. No sensible mind will say, either, that the King has commanded the Parlement or the inhabitants of Paris impossible things, which must have been done to render this necessity absolute, the only condition which could in any way excuse you before men, but not before God, who commands us, being persecuted in one city, to flee to another."

This writer's thought is probably that of the author of the *Christian and Political Answer to the Erroneous Opinions of the Time*,[28] who allows disobedience to royal commands in violation of divine law. The passage in point is the reply to the proposition, *That one is not obliged to obey the King if he does not command justly*. It reads: "It is true that if the King should command to reject the Mass, to quit the Sacraments, to seduce and violate women, in that case one should not obey him, since it is contrary to divine law, but as regards the Civil Laws, one must obey with bowed head and closed eyes, since God commands us to obey the superior powers, not only good princes, but also bad ones."

There were some who found this doctrine too liberal, and declared that the obligation of obedience is unlimited. Among these is the author of the most famous government pamphlet of the second phase of the Fronde, the *Sentiments of a Faithful Subject of the King*.[29] Resting on the authority of Pope John VIII, the sixth Council of Paris, and especially Saint Augustine, he says: "In the thought of Saint Augustine there is no vice, nor infidelity, nor apostasy, nor severity of government, which can dispense us from the fidelity or obedience which we have promised to our legitimate Sovereigns."

The obligations of obedience and non-resistance are, we have seen, based upon revelation. Many of these writers are content to cite their authority, Scripture, or the teaching of the Church, without explaining it. Two attempts at explanation, however, were made: one is, that God has reserved to Himself the punish-

---

[28] *Response chrestienne et politique*, etc.
[29] *Les sentimens d'un fidelle suiet du Roy*, etc.

ment of wicked princes;[30] the other, that the wicked prince is the instrument of God's wrath. The second idea is expressed in the following passage from the *Refutation of the Lettre d'Avis:*[31] "If we do not consider them (Kings) as celestial favors, as Solomon compares them in their sweetness to the cloud which bears the agreeable dew of the evening: We ought always to consider them as illustrious Barbarians, before whom we must not play the magnificent: as flails of Heaven, whom we must not resist, but whom we should pray God to soften. Just as truly as good Kings are presents of the rarest goodness of God, it must not be doubted that the violent are his chastisements and severest punishments. But if they are rods in the hand of God, are we permitted to break them if he chastises us for our offenses?"

This passage comes very close to advocacy of tyranny: if the acts of the wicked prince are willed by God, they must be good. It is probable, however that the author would have shrunk from this conclusion, and attempted to reconcile condemnation of tyranny with the theory that the tyrant is an instrument of God. This seems to have been the thought of the author of the *Very Humble Remonstrance to the Prince of Condé.*[32] He says: "In fact they (Kings) are Lieutenants of an independent virtue, before whom we must not play the wise nor the magnificent. They are scourges which we have asked of God, which he has given us in His indignation, to punish us for our crimes. They are sacred thunderbolts in the hand of that terrible Jupiter, to whom we shall some day be obliged to render account of all our actions, and which we must revere as his Living Images. . . . As often as the Monarch takes pains to correct us, so often are we obliged to kiss the rod with which he punishes us. . . . It is true that if their power has no limits as regards us, it nevertheless has limits as regards Him who will examine severely even the least of their thoughts. . . . Was not Jeroboam threatened with a very horrible death for having illtreated his people? . . . Holy Writ is only too fertile in examples of this nature, which show us

[30] See the *Image du souverain*, etc.

[31] *Responce et refutation du discours intitulé Lettre d'Avis*, etc.

[32] *Très-humble remontrance faite à monsieur le prince de Condé*, etc.

that His Divine Majesty does not pardon them any more than the rest of His creatures. It is from Him, then, that you must await the justice of your cause."

The principles set forth above were, I believe, those of the great majority of the supporters of the government. They may, perhaps, be summarized as follows: The King monopolizes all constituted civil power; the other authorities of the kingdom, if they are not his delegates, cannot disobey his command. But although alone in the government of the state, he is nevertheless limited: he is bound by reason and justice, and by the will of God as revealed in Scripture and the teaching of the Church. If he oversteps the limits of his power, it is doubtful if there is any remedy except prayer; the most that can be allowed is passive resistance to a command which contradicts the expressed will of God.

But if this was the doctrine of the majority of the party of the government, there were some who went much farther. There is evidence that it was held that the power of the King was above justice and reason.

This is usually expressed in the proposition: The King is master of the goods and lives of his subjects. Claude Joly devotes a long passage in the *Maxims*[33] to a refutation of this thesis, and it is dealt with in many of the opposition pamphlets, including one of the best, the *Lettre d'Avis*.[34] The passage in point in this pamphlet reads as follows: "Detestable thieves have tried for thirty years to get us to accept a tyrannical politics, and have published everywhere that the King has the right of life and death over his subjects, that our lives and our goods are his, and that he can dispose of them as he likes, being the Sovereign Master. It is true that subjects are naturally obligated to employ their lives and their goods for the service of their Prince: but there is great difference between these two propositions: the Prince can take and dispose of our lives and our goods at his fantasy, and we ought to employ lives and goods for the Prince. The first supposes a Despotic and Seignorial power; and the

---

[33] Joly, *Recueil de maximes*, etc., in Chapter XI.
[34] *Lettre d'avis à messieurs du Parlement de Paris*, etc.

second a subjection in the subject which obliges him to serve his Prince at the expense of his blood and his goods, when the need is great. France has never been a despotic government, unless it be in the last thirty years, when we have been subject to the mercy of Ministers and exposed to their tyranny. . . . France is a pure Royal Monarchy, in which the Prince is obliged to conform to the laws of God, and where his people, obeying him, remain in natural liberty and property in their goods: while the Despotic governs subjects as a father of a family his slaves."

Though this evidence is from the other side, it is sufficient proof: the tone of the *Lettre d'Avis* rings true, and the character of Joly makes it unthinkable that he would set up a man of straw. It will be remembered, too, that Le Bret found it necessary to refute certain old writers who had taught that the King is master of the goods of his subjects. But open defense of this thesis is very rare. I have found it in only two publications of the controversy, the *Reply of Father Faure*,[35] and the *Veritable Censure of the Lettre d'Avis*.[36]   52298

The passage in point from the first of these works is as follows: "And now, Reverend Father, what do you think of these words? (First Kings, 11-17) Will you, as you say, buck against the goad? Is it not true that here is the evidence, the force, the domination, and the Seignory of everything which a Kingdom can contain? Will you maintain that our goods, our blood, and even our lives are not under the absolute power of the King . . . ? The King is the master and not the valet: he can tear down and build up: he can absolve and punish: he can put a bit in the mouth of his peoples and drive them (*les mener à courbet*), exactly as he pleases." The passage from the *Veritable Censure of the Lettre d'Avis* reads: "Judge from that (the establishment of Saul), I beg of you, if Subjects have the right to oppose the authority of their Sovereigns, since they have received them from the hand of this All Powerful only under the conditions which we have just stated. . . . That shows you clearly, Sir, that Kings have a power so sovereign over their Subjects that they have only to

[35] *La Response du père Favre*, etc.
[36] *Véritable censure de la Lettre d'avis*, etc.

choose, with extreme resolution, either death or obedience. Holy
Writ is fertile enough in examples of this nature. . . . The infinite Wisdom teaches us in the eighth chapter of His Ecclesiastes,
that the King can do with us anything that he pleases, without
any exception."

2. THEORY OF ABSOLUTISM

We will show in the sixth chapter that the case of the opposition rests upon the constitution, the traditional form of the state.
That of the apologists of the government, on the other hand,
rests not upon the constitution, but upon "reason," backed by
Scriptural or ecclesiastical authority.

This is true even of the lawyer Le Bret. He mentions, it is
true, in two places, "the Ordinance of Charles VIII," which gives
complete authority to the King in matters of state. One of these
references we have already seen; it occurs in his discussion of
Article 98 of the Ordinance of Blois: "Since he has reserved to
himself the cognizance of these matters (public affairs, and which
touch the State) according to the Edict of Charles VIII, he can
commit such persons as he pleases to have cognizance of them."[37]
The second is in Chapter 14; it reads: "The Parlement formerly
had the custom of granting Letters of Marque. But that was in
the time when our Kings visited their Parlement more often, and
went there to take counsel in the great affairs of the Kingdom:
for since the Ordinance of Charles VIII, and since the Kings who
have come after him have reserved to themselves cognizance of
the affairs of their State, it is only they who grant them."[38] He
does not quote this ordinance, nor give the title or date.

The constitutional reference in Le Bret is little more than a
bow to the traditional form of political argumentation. And this
is exceptional: none of the government writers of the controversy,
whom I have read, so much as mentions the constitution; there
are some, in fact, who attack constitutionalism.

Among these is the author of the *Christian and Political Answer*

[37] Le Bret, *De la Souveraineté du Roy*, 151.
[38] Le Bret, *De la Souveraineté du Roy*, 302.

to the Erroneous Opinions of the Time.[39] The passage has already been quoted: ". . . those who want to speak of the power of the ancient Kings of France, and of their way of acting, to draw consequences for the present time, would be guilty of putting forward a seditious and pernicious proposition, as if it were said that the King ought to share France, and divide it into four Kingdoms, because Clovis, the first Christian King did it, and several Kings after him." In the *Veritable Censure of the Lettre d'Avis*[40] constitutionalism is rejected as impious. This writer says: "You are as bad a Christian as Politician. For if you have the right to draw your conclusions from a Merovée, whom subjects raised to this Royal dignity, it seems to me that I shall have much more to draw mine from a Saul, whom God took care to crown Himself with His own hand, wicked as he was, over a people whom he cherished above all others. Things done by this Sovereign Lord, should have more credit in the minds of men, than anything His creatures can do; and His promotions are of a much more stable nature, and more important than ours, without any contradiction."

Absolutism, then, did not rest upon the law. The theoretical bases of the doctrine are expressed in the following passage from the *Christian and Political Answer.*[41] It is part of the author's reply to the proposition, *That Kings ought not to have absolute power, since it degenerates ordinarily into tyranny.* "Sovereigns," he says, "who bear on earth the living reflection of this divine Original, in the care which they take to govern the people which God has submitted to them, will they be different from the pattern upon which they have been made? Will they not have also an absolute power over those who ought to obey them, since it is impossible to rule and govern the commonwealth (*la chose publique*) well, without this sovereign and absolute power? For if there were resistance to command, and in obedience Discernment, everything would fall into disorder and confusion, and everyone would explain the Will of the Prince according to his fantasy:

---

[39] *Response chrestienne et politique*, etc.
[40] *Véritable censure de la Lettre d'avis*, etc.
[41] *Response chrestienne et politique*, etc.

that is why it is necessary in all states that the absolute power should be in the hands of someone, that there should be a Command in last appeal, which is sovereign, and absolute, to prevent the disorders of the State of Nature, which is a war of all against all, because of the equal power that everyone possesses. In Democracy this power is in the people; in Aristocracy in the Senate; and in Monarchy in the King: and that absolute power is indivisible, even in the States where there is some temperament, for if some dispute arises, it must necessarily be settled by the authority of the people or of the senate or of the King, otherwise there would be no Sovereignty in any state whatsoever, together with the fact that if it comes to that, either there will be no end to the dispute, which will be the universal ruin of the State, or it will be ended only by the destruction of one of the parties, after a long Civil war, which would be even a greater ruin and desolation: for to say that the Law will have this absolute power is an error, since in all differences everyone alleges the Law and pulls it to his side, and someone must necessarily cry halt, and force adherence to what he says and commands, or everything will fall into confusion, and everybody be master and fight for place (*ioüe au boute dehors, à qui sera plus fort*) like the beasts. In what place is the word of the King, there is the power, says Ecclesiastes, and who will say to him, What art thou doing? That is why no one can control his commands and his actions without making a breach in sovereignty, and so alter the State, which is the true tyranny; for the greatest and most excellent public good is that which regards the conservation of the authority of the Prince, as the greatest and most pernicious evil which can be imagined, is to encroach upon his authority, and to attribute to oneself the sovereign power which belongs to him alone, though he use it to molest and afflict his subjects; for all the Histories show us that the trouble which has been given Princes by resisting obedience, however wicked they have been, has brought the public more harm than their bad government, since (*d'autant*) in disobeying them one disobeys God, who has ordered by express words to obey the powers: and so the power of Princes over their Subjects is of divine right, since it obligates the soul which has only God as supreme legislator. And so Saint Jerome says, one must be faithful and obedient to the Principalities, otherwise no one can hope for salvation from God."

It will have been noticed that this writer appears to put monarchy, aristocracy, and democracy on the same plane. But that this was not his thought is apparent in another passage where he says that of the three forms of government monarchy is the best "because of Unity, and because more like God, who willed to be born of the blood of crowned heads."

In admitting the possibility of aristocracy and democracy the *Christian and Political Answer* is exceptional. To most of these writers, monarchy is the only form of government. The following passage from the *Answer and Refutation of the Lettre d'Avis*[42] is typical of their pronouncements on this subject: "Whatever opinion you have of Sovereignty, Sir, I believe that you do not doubt that it ought to reign everywhere. If you consider the Universe in its entirety, you will see there a Sovereign and universal power, upon which depend all the others. If you divide it into world intelligible and world corporeal, you find again a supreme intelligence over all the inferior, and a sublime body over all those which are below it. If you divide the world into Kingdoms or Republics, each one of them has its Sovereignty; the Kingdoms into Provinces, they have their Governors; the Provinces into Cities, they have their Justices; the Cities into houses, their fathers of families.

"This generality of examples, Sir, is an infallible mark of the necessity of Sovereign power for the universal government of all things; and I have often wondered that several wise Republics have attempted to subsist in the nullification of this power: to speak as the matter deserves, it is to found one's establishment on a base of ruin, and to break one's ship to pieces, in order to make the journey more easily. For if one is not to err, for the good of States, the stronger this power and the better accepted, the more useful and harmonious it is. But to give it its entire vigor, it must be placed in a subject, be rendered indivisible in his person, by this person only communicable to those who are

---

[42] *Responce et refutation du discours intitulé Lettre d'Avis*, etc.

established to help him. The subject, then, where this Power must reside is that which we call Monarch. It is thus that the universal government is in the hands of God, who is the only Sovereign of the Universe, and who dominates all the world, independent of all other beings. On this model, not only beautiful, but also good, and the most perfect that can teach us, all sorts of governments must pattern themselves; from this it comes too that all wise Politicians have been able to comprehend no other perfect government than the Royal Monarchical: because it is the only one imitated from an infallible original. . . . The reason for this is beautiful and very easy to understand: it is, that in the division of power discord never fails to be found: and it is the ruin of all things. . . . The government of a single just Monarch is then infallibly the only one which conforms with the laws of the Universe."

The reason for this insistence upon undivided absolute authority is the natural wickedness of man. We saw in the *Christian and Political Answer* that the state of nature is a war of all against all. This idea is developed as follows in the *Image of the Sovereign:*[43] "The third reason why Kings were created was a necessity of self preservation, which led the people to seek a way whereby they might correct the fury and oppression of the wicked, since we are naturally inclined to do evil, and since there are always some so vicious that by their malice they trouble and ruin all human order. . . . So that to prevent these disorders they were obliged to create a chief who would command all, and who could preserve the good in possession of their own property, and punish the wicked, to exterminate their race. This sole reason obliges us to believe that Kings were established from the beginning of the world, and almost immediately after our first Fathers were banished from the earthly Paradise."

But this utilitarian argument is dangerous: if obedience rests only on public convenience, it might be maintained that there are circumstances in which the public would profit from revolt. Most of the absolutists, consequently, as we have already seen, hasten to bolster up the utilitarian argument with sacred au-

[43] *L'Image du souverain*, etc.

thority. The author of the pamphlet last cited insists that though the King exists for the people, and may have been elected by them, he nevertheless holds his power directly from God. The passage reads: "It remains to be verified, by whom Kings were created, which is a matter in which most of the world goes astray. I say to begin with, that no one can deny that it is from God that Kings hold their Sceptre and their Crown, since He is the author of all things. And everybody should know that the subjects of the Monarchs do not contribute in any way to their election, and that they are Sovereigns established by that infinite Forseer, to render Justice to peoples. When they recognize him as their Prince, they do only what they are obligated to do." The *Answer and Refutation of the Lettre d'Avis*[44] says: "It must be understood that it is never the Subjects who make the King. When they elect him, it is indeed a mark of his legitimate vocation, but not of the power of those who elect him." The best statement on this point is in the *Christian and Political Answer:*[45] "It is certain that Kings are established by God for the people, but it is as the Soul is created for the body, and the Head for the members, and the Shepherd for the flock, that is to say, in a superior degree, to lead and command, and not to put the feet over the head. . . . Besides, the King does not swear to obey the people as a body or individually, but indeed the whole people as a body and individually swear to obey the King, and obligate themselves at the time of the Consecration by a new oath: For they are already obligated by Divine Law and the Law of Nature, and so it is only a public recognition and profession of this obligation: The King does not obligate himself, then, either, to render justice to his subjects and to command them as he should, he is also obligated to do this by the same Divine Law at the time that the succession to the Kingdom falls to him, but he merely gives this public evidence of his obligation; all the Grandees of the Kingdom, all the Magistrates, all the Prelates and Officers of the Crown promise fidelity and obedience to the King, as to their sovereign Lord, to whom God gave command when He said: By

[44] *Responce et refutation du discours intitulé Lettre d'Avis*, etc.
[45] *Response chrestienne et politique*, etc.

Me reign the Kings: and to the people obedience and subjection, Obey and be subjects in all fear to your Masters, etc. When
this is practised, Kingdoms are happy, for on the peace of the
Prince depends that of the subjects, as Solomon said, together
with the fact that if the people were above the King, all domination would be Democratic."

The state, a product of the wickedness of man, will have as its
principle, not justice and reason, but order. We saw in the
Christian and Political Answer that "the greatest and most excellent public good is that which regards the conservation of the
authority of the Prince, as the greatest and most pernicious evil
which can be imagined is to encroach upon his authority." The
Prince, confronted by a choice between justice and his security,
which is that of the state, will prefer his security; he will act not
according to reason, but according to *reason of state*.

The expression *raison d'état* appears frequently in the writings
of the defenders of the government. It is defined as follows in
the *Political Considerations on Coups d'État*, an earlier work of
one of the leading government apologists, Mazarin's librarian,
Gabriel Naudé: *Coups d'État* or *Raison d' État*, are "hardy and
extraordinary actions which Princes are forced to execute in difficult and, shall we say, desperate conjunctures against common
law, without even keeping any order or form of justice, risking
the interest of the individual for the good of the public."[46] The
"law," *salus populi suprema lex esto*, he goes on to say, absolves
Princes "from many little circumstances and formalities, to which
justice obligates them: Thus they are masters of the laws to
lengthen them or to shorten them, not as they please, but as
reason and public utility permit; the honor of the Prince, the
love of country, the safety of the people certainly counterbalance
a few small faults and injustices; and we would apply again the
saying of the Prophet, if it can be done without being profane:
Expedit ut unus homo moriatur pro populo, ne tota gens pereat."[47]

Instead of *reason of state*, the expression *mystery of state* is
sometimes used. This seems to have had two meanings, corre-

[46] Naudé, *Considerations Politiques sur les Coups d'Estat*, 65.
[47] Naudé, *Considerations Politiques sur les Coups d'Estat*, 77-78.

sponding to the two bases of the absolutistic doctrine, reason and religion. To the mystics, mystery of state is faith in the divine inspiration of the Prince. Divinely inspired, his motives are unknowable to men; though he may perform acts contrary to justice and reason, those acts are good, since they are done by God. This has appeared in the passages above, in which obedience to a tyrant is advocated on the ground that he is the instrument of the vengeance of God.

The superhumanity of the King is asserted in many of the works written for the government. Le Bret held this belief. Speaking of the majority of the King of France at the age of fourteen, he says: "It has often been noticed that these sacred persons, by a special favor of Heaven, are ordinarily enriched from an early age with several virtues and fine qualities, which are not met with in other and lower conditions."[48] And in another place he speaks of the miraculous effects of consecration: "Our Kings, being anointed at their consecration with that miraculous liquor which Heaven has given them, to serve them in this solemn act, are enriched by its virtue with so many extraordinary favors, that they seem to be raised to a condition quite divine: they cure the most baneful diseases by their mere touch; they are so strengthened in heart and courage that wherever they appear they bring terror to their enemies."[49]

To the rationalists the mystery of state is not a mystery of religion, but of science. This idea is clearly expressed in an opposition pamphlet, the *Summary of the Curious Doctrine of Cardinal Mazarin*.[50] In answer to the question, *What are the maxims which you made use of to administer the State*, Mazarin is made to reply: "I have already declared a part of them. . . . As for the others, they depend upon secret Politics which for the good of the state should be kept hidden, because it would seem more unbearable to the people, who are not versed in this science, concerning which I have abstained from speaking in my Answers, though it would have served me to justify my actions and my

[48] Le Bret, *De la Souveraineté du Roy*, in Chapter V.
[49] Le Bret, *De la Souveraineté du Roy*, 122-123.
[50] *Sommaire de la doctrine curieuse du cardinal Mazarin*, etc.

conduct." In another place in this pamphlet Mazarin says: "I should not be blamed for having pronounced this condemnation without investigation and without form, since being the representative of the person of the Prince, I possess in myself dispensation from all the Laws and Ordinances of the Kingdom, which are established only for the direction of ordinary Judges, and common minds; so that they, who do not possess this infallibility of judgment, which is the property (*partage*) of great minds, may find an order in these formalities to aid their deliberations." The government apologists did not hesitate to adopt this argument. One of them wrote in the *Reply to the Political Resolution of the two Principal Doubts:*[51] "Reason of state or Political prudence is so difficult to understand that the life of man is too short to understand it, and you, Monsieur the critic, who have perhaps never put your nose elsewhere than in a class of Pedantry, want to put yourself forward and give lessons to the most completely versed (*aux plus consommez*) in all that this science contains of mysterious, and in the resolution and demonstration of the most difficult things." Mazarin is past master in this science: "Let people like you criticize the Ministry of his Eminence, but at the same time let them propose a man better grounded than he is in the reason of State and in Political science."

There is evidence that some would have agreed with the statement of the principles of this science made by Naudé in a chapter entitled, *Of what opinions one must be persuaded to undertake Coups d' ̂tat*. One of these is, that the populace is stupid. He says: "I say that the populace is inferior to the beasts, worse than the beasts, and more stupid a hundred times than the beasts themselves; for the beasts, not having the use of reason, allow themselves to be conducted by instinct, which Nature gives them as a rule of life, of their actions, passions, and conduct, from which they never deviate. . . ." The populace, on the contrary, "being endowed with reason, abuses it in a thousand ways, and becomes by means of this the Theater where the orators, the preachers, the false Prophets, the impostors, the seditious, the malcontent, the superstitious, the ambitious, in brief all who have some new

[51] *Réponse à la résolution politique*, etc.

design, play their most furious and bloody tragedies. . . . But since force is always on their side, and since it is the populace which gives the greatest movement (*bransle*) to everything extraordinary that happens in the State, it is necessary for Princes or their Ministers to study to manage and persuade it by fine words, seduce and deceive it by appearances, win it and turn it to their designs by preachers and miracles under the pretext of sanctity, or by means of good pens, having them write clandestine pamphlets, manifestoes, apologies, and declarations artistically composed, to lead it by the nose, and have it approve or condemn what the sack contains by the label on the outside. . . . I must show how Princes or their Ministers, *quibus quaestui sunt capti superstitione animi*, have contrived to exploit (*ménager*) Religion and use it as the easiest and most certain means they have to come to the end of their more exalted enterprises."[52]

The argument for absolutism, as it appears in most of the defenses of the government, may, it would seem, be summarized as follows: Sprung from the instinct of self preservation, the end of the state is peace. Peace can be obtained only by the award of unlimited power to a single person. But this, if reasonable, is

[52] Naudé, *Considerations Politiques sur les Coups d'Estat*, 153-161.

Comparable sentiments are expressed in the literature of the Fronde. The following passage is from the *Response au Réveille-matin de la Fronde royalle*, etc. "Don't be astonished if he (Mazarin) breaks his word every time he negotiates; there is no one who can say that a King is obligated to keep the oaths which he makes to his subjects, especially when he is obliged to make them to improve his affairs. . . . Oaths assume a certain equality of condition, and a kind of independence." See also *Le caractère du royaliste à Agathon*.

A great many of the opposition writers accuse the government of perfidy. The charge was made officially in a Parlementary remonstrance of March, 1652. The passage in point reads: "But the most detestable and dangerous Favorites of Kings are those who, after having counseled them to use perfidy to get out of certain difficult situations, are so malicious as to attempt to establish it by general maxims, and so audacious as to make them public. Cardinal Mazarin who has practised them, has also taught them, having several times said that good faith should be in use only among Merchants, that a gentleman (*l'honneste homme*) is not the slave of his word, and that there is no danger in lying, provided the lie is not known until after it has succeeded. If these damnable lessons enter the soul of a Prince of your age, what remedies shall we find for a civil or a foreign war?" *Journal du Parlement*, at the date March 23, 1652.

also the will of God, as revealed in the Bible and the doctrine of the Church.

But this summary is not quite complete. We have seen one statement which implies an end for the state beyond peace. Naudé, it will be remembered, justified *coups d'état* by appealing to the "honor of the Prince" and the "love of country" as well as the safety of the people. These phrases, and the word "glory," are not uncommon in the government writings. Le Bret considers "honor" a respectable motive; a passage in his book reads: "I cannot omit saying that if there is any occasion when the ambassador should show his courage and generosity, it is principally when it is a question of keeping his rank and precedence (*séance*): for there is nothing that Princes and sovereign states are more jealous of or eager for than the conservation of this honor."[53] Beyond peace, the end of the state is honor and glory, which is prestige through power.

To some, glory is shared by the people, as the triumph of the general is shared by his soldiers, but others seem to have held that the people are too low spirited for such motives. One writer says that glory is a sentiment "too refined for common minds," and this was the secret opinion of Naudé. To these persons, the state is the instrument of the glory of the prince, a concept which rests finally upon conviction of the moral grandeur of the lust for power, and admiration for the science of domination. This appears in many places in Naudé's book; it is implicit in the phrase, "their more exalted enterprises," quoted above. It is clear in a passage in which he agrees with the "atheists" that Moses threw himself down some precipice, and finds the act admirable because of the loftiness of the goal: "immortality." This idea I have seen somewhere expressed in the form of a maxim: "Everything is permitted to one who would rule" (*On peut tout faire pour regner*).

[53] Le Bret, *De la Souveraineté du Roy*, 601-602.

CHAPTER V

DEFENSE OF THE OPPOSITION (I)

THE public declarations of the opposition, which we examined in the first section of Chapter III, indicate that they held that the King was not alone in the government, but shared the power of the state with other authorities. This conclusion is confirmed, as we shall see, by the great majority of the works written in defense of the opposition; it is stated clearly in several of them, where it is said that the Kingdom of France is not fully monarchical.

But there was one important pronouncement of the Parlement which could hardly be reconciled with this conclusion, the remonstrances of January 21st, 1649. There the Court, while declaring that the King must do justice, and that resistance by the people under certain circumstances is permissible, imply that he is alone in the state. This stand is taken by a small minority of the defenders of the opposition. Our examination of the defense of the opposition will begin with these works.

1. THE MONARCHY LIMITED BY LAW AND THE RIGHT OF RESISTANCE

That the King is bound by justice as well as by divine law is stated or implied by all these writers. The following passage is from the *Political Theologian*:[1] "Kings and Princes, although they call themselves independent . . . are subject to the divine laws and to those of natural equity printed in the hearts of all men: and the Edicts and Ordinances which they give their subjects are, or ought to be, only the expositions of these laws."

The *Catechism of the Partisans*[2] deals as follows with the form-

---

[1] *Le Théologien politique*, etc.
[2] *Catéchisme des partisans*, etc.

ula, the King is master of the lives and goods of his subjects. To
the question, *Is the King master of the life of his subjects*, the reply
is made: "Yes, but not in the manner that the Politics of Machia-
velli has it, but in that which we learn from the Gospel, that is
to say, the King, exercising the justice of God over men, has the
right to take their lives or to save them, in conformity with the
laws of God and not otherwise, or with those which he has established, and which do not derogate from those of God, if he would
not sin . . . for Kings are not of themselves absolute and independent; only God possesses this perfection. . . . It is for this
reason that in the Old Testament it was established that the
King should take the book of the law from the hand of the Priest;
and in that of the New Alliance the King is made to kiss the book
of the Gospel when he is present at the august sacrifice of the
Body of Jesus Christ, to show him the obligation he is under to
follow the orders of God and the Gospel. . . . Thus the right of
life and death which the Sovereign has over his subjects, ought
to be regulated by the divine and infallible rules, when it is a
question either of avenging crimes or of pardoning the guilty.
And it is on this foundation that Saint Paul asserts that they are
redoubtable, not having uselessly the sword in hand; and that
the Chancellor refuses to seal letters of grace when he sees that
they are not in the order of Justice."

Immediately after this passage the author deals with property.
The question is put as follows: "If there are limits to the power
of Kings as regards the lives of men, are there any also in regard
to their faculties? Is not the King master of all the goods of his
Subjects? Has he not the right to dispose of them as he pleases,
without other motive or consideration than his will alone? So
that if he should take everything, he would only be making use
of his right, and if he leaves anything, it is favor and alms, for
which one is obligated to him, and to which he was not obligated?" The answer is: "Not at all. Those are impious, damnable, and abominable maxims, which could be approved or authorized only among the most barbarous and degenerate peoples. . . . One should reason, then, on goods, in the same way,
and in proportion, as on lives, and put everywhere the laws of

God, of the Gospel, and of Charity, like a torch to serve as a guide to escape the reefs and precipices which are met in the exercise of the Sovereign power." The true Christian law on this subject is that the King can take his people's goods only for the public service: "Since the property of the people does not belong to the King, he cannot take it except to provide for necessity, and not more."

The same doctrine is set forth in the *Political Theologian.*[3] The passage reads: "As for our goods and our lives, no one doubts that they can be the Dispensers, provided, nevertheless, that it be for the glory of God, the good of the Public, and that they be employed with a just and legitimate moderation for the conservation of the State, and that they be not exacted to satisfy the avidity, ambition, and cruelty of Favorites and a thousand other bloodsuckers who surround Princes."

The right of private property is stated as follows in the *Christian and Political Discourse on the Power of Kings:*[4] "Everything is the King's as far as the Sovereign authority is concerned, although property in goods belongs to each individual. *Singulae res, singulorum sunt*, this maxim is indubitable, it is recognized throughout the world, and Emperors though Pagan have not questioned it."

It will have been noticed that the author of the *Catechism of the Partisans* founds his doctrine on divine law, but neglects to cite his texts. In the *Political Theologian* and the *Christian and Political Discourse on the Power of Kings* quotations from Plato and Aristotle are mingled with Scripture. The thought of these men, and it was very common, seems to be that reason is divine. Though revelation is above reason, it does not abrogate it, but fulfills it.

We have as yet heard little of the laws and customs of the Kingdom. It is very improbable, however, that these writers would have denied that the "civil law" is binding. I have, in fact, found only one opposition work in which this is doubted. That

---

[3] *Le Théologien politique*, etc.

[4] *Discours chrestien et politique*, etc.

is the *True Courtier without Flattery*.[5] The passage reads: "If the authority of Kings is above the laws, it is only above the civil, because it is this authority which promulgates them, and which is the cause of them; but it is not above the laws which Nature prescribes, and which the Divinity commands, recognizing above itself an Author of these Laws, to whom the King cannot call himself equal except criminally, and without reason. And those who call it (the royal authority) independent of these Laws do it evil, since, attempting to carry it too high, and above the Divinity Himself, they are the source of its ruin. They are wrong to say that it is independent, since Christianity is above, and since it follows its laws with veneration and obligation."

The King is bound to do justice. If he fails in his duty, these writers declare or imply that it is legitimate for the people to resist him. In the following passage from the *Moral and Christian Maxims*[6] disobedience is allowed when the King commands things opposed to salvation. The author begins by affirming the obligation of obedience: "The royal authority being of divine institution, though several Kings are only of that of men, this character of the majesty of God which they bear with such brilliance, requires necessarily from their subjects respect in conformity with this grandeur." But he immediately adds that the obedience which is due Kings is limited: "From this first maxim comes the second, which is the obedience which is owed the King, which is not blind, as some attempt falsely to maintain, but in conformity with the laws of God, the rules of the Gospel, and of the Catholic, Apostolic and Roman Church; for as Kings are the Lieutenants of God for the temporal guidance of men, it is from Him and not from themselves that they should take the Laws and Ordinances necessary for their conservation; and since the soul is more precious than the body, and the interest of salvation preferable to that of fortune, the maxims of our Religion ought to be the rules of Politics; so that, so long as Kings command things which are not opposed to salvation, subjects are bound to obey; but as soon as they pass the boundaries, Saint Peter

[5] *Le vray courtisan sans flaterie*, etc.
[6] *Maximes morales et chrestiennes*, etc.

teaches us the reply which we ought to make: that there is no reason (*apparence*) to render obedience to men to the prejudice of that which we owe God."

Whether this writer would have allowed resistance, and to commands contrary to "justice," may be doubted, though we have seen divine law extended to include reason. But there is no doubt of the meaning of the authors of the *Political Theologian* and the *Christian and Political Discourse on the Power of Kings.* The first says: "It is not permitted Kings to do all they want, but only all that is just, and profitable to the Peoples over whom God has established them . . . if Kings contravene what they are obligated to do for their subjects, it is without doubt permitted subjects, by a relative equity, not to render an unjust obedience, which they exact from cruelty rather than by just mildness. . . ." The *Christian and Political Discourse* begins with citations from the Bible to prove that Kings are elected and deposed by the people, and ends with a grim warning: "Let the Great show their faith by their works: or let them no longer demand of us reverence for their dignity. Let them cease in their own interest to abandon everything to force, which is doubtless on the side of the greater number."

The most complete exposition of this doctrine of limited monarchy is contained in a pamphlet entitled *Reasonable Complaint against the last Declaration of the King.*[7] I shall quote it at length.

The author begins with the problem of resistance: "And first, all disobedience is not rebellion. If the Prince or his Minister commands a thing contrary to the law of God, refusal to Obey is neither rebellion nor crime; on the contrary, it would be a crime to obey: *Sperne potestatem timendo potestatem*, says Saint Augustine; that is to say, thou canst with impunity, indeed thou shouldst despise the command of human power to satisfy that of the All Powerful. Second, if the Prince gives you a command which in itself is not against the law of God, but nevertheless is unjust, because it is excessive, in that case it is the Prince who sins, because he acts against the law of God, which obligates him to do justice; but thou, in executing it, dost not offend; on the

[7] *Le raisonnable plaintif sur la dernière déclaration du roy.*

contrary thou exercisest patience. But this patience is praiseworthy; and resistance, on the contrary, would be useless, would
be of bad example, and injurious to thee. In this case thou must
obey; and the Magistrate who acts under the authority of the
Prince can force thee by fines, pains, and imprisonments. And
though the imposition be excessive and in itself unjust, nevertheless in consideration of the public peace, which thou shouldst not
trouble by thy impatience, it is just that thou shouldst bear it.
But if the charge and the *corvée* are universally imposed on all the
inhabitants of the country, and being unable to bear it longer,
they resolve to refuse it, and if in vengeance for this refusal they
are proceeded against by outrages and declared war, if they are
starved, if they are massacred, if their wives and daughters are
violated, nature then rises against the pretended civil law which
the Prince alleges (*se veut prévaloir*) and opposes the shield of
legitimate defense to force and violence: *Vim vi defendere omnes
leges et omnia iura permittunt.* For then, respect being lost on the
part of the people, and the Prince having stripped himself of all
charity, and giving no longer justice or protection, the mutual tie
is dissolved; there is no longer either Prince or subjects; and
things are reduced to their first condition (*à la matière première*).
Then it happens that the form of the government changes entirely; for either the Monarchy passes into Aristocracy or into a
popular state; or if the people are not entirely disgusted with
Royalty, they transfer it to another family, or they submit to
another, more powerful nation, and ruled by better laws."

He then proceeds to prove that this doctrine is in conformity
with revelation, attacking the interpretation made by the absolutists of the thirteenth chapter of the Epistle to the Romans,
and of Saint Peter's affirmation of the duty of obedience. His
comment on the latter is as follows: "And when Saint Peter commands Servitors to obey their Masters, *etiam dyscolis*, this word
means only when they are morose and in bad humor. It is a
different matter when they kill and massacre; then this obligation is no longer within its limits. Then nature declares herself,
and takes for herself legitimate defense, and tramples under foot
the pretended civil law, just as do those trained lions, when they

have suffered from their masters some great outrage which exhausts their patience and docility. That is just what has happened in our days in several provinces of Europe."

Having thus dealt with the problem of resistance, this author turns next to an examination of the nature of the state, appealing to reason and the authority of the classical philosophers. The passage is as follows: "And first Polybius will teach them (favorites and proponents of absolutism) that there is a notable distinction to be made between Monarchy and Royalty. The latter is a legitimate power accorded by the will and choice of the people. Monarchy is a violent power which dominates against the will of subjects, and which has subjected them against their will. Royalty governs itself by reason; Monarchy by whim (*à discretion*) and according to the covetousness of the commander. The end of Royalty is the common good; the end of the Monarch is his own. Aristotle, king of minds and human reason, says that monarchical government, that is to say, of a single person, is bestial like that of the King of the bees, who rules them without counsel; that Royalty is a government proper for men, which is administered by counsel and by communication of the opinions of capable persons. Cicero, the prince of Latin philosophers, as well as orators, says after Aristotle, and with the approval of all Politicians, that peoples have elected Kings to do them justice and to protect them; that for this purpose they have chosen the most virtuous and the wisest. And if Cicero, Polybius and Aristotle had not said it, can it enter common sense that they could have done otherwise? These same great geniuses tell us that the governors of peoples and republics, whether Kings, Emperors, Electors, Consuls, or called by whatever other names, ought to be considered in no other way than tutors in regard to their pupils: *Ut tutela, sic procuratio reipublicae, ad eorum utilitatem qui commissi sunt, non ad eorum quibus commissa est, referenda est.* This oracle is so useful, so beautiful, and of such indubitable virtue, that it should be inscribed in the palaces of all Princes, in all court rooms, and in all meeting places of public councils. Fabius Maximus, according to Livy, when Scipio the Younger wanted to transport his army to Africa against the will of the Senate, set forth his opinion in these terms: I think, elected Fathers (*Peres conscrits*) that Scipio has been created consul for the good of the republic and for ours, and not for his own. The same can be said to all who have been given power to govern a nation, whatever the names with which they are honored."

That the end of the state is justice is immediately apparent to common sense and is taught by the great philosophers. But if this is reasonable, it is also a fundamental principle of the French kingdom. The following passage comes immediately after the last one quoted: "Just as this consul or this dictator is obligated to rule himself by justice during his year or his six months, the King likewise is obligated to administer justice during the whole course of his life and his reign. They have never been elected under other conditions; and it is impossible to conceive that a community however barbarous, has created for itself a chief to be afflicted and curbed by him. This being so, of whatever date is the origin of a Monarchy, it cannot prescribe the liberty of a nation which has given it being and beginning. It is a maxim indubitable in Law, and which lawyers (*les gens de robbe*) ought not to be ignorant of, that *nemo potest sibi mutare causam possessionis*. Hugh Capet was elected by the Estates of France to reign equitably and according to the laws of the country; he made a solemn oath to do it at the time of his consecration; he consequently transmitted the kingdom to his posterity on the same condition. If Louis XI attempted things beyond this, he sinned against his duty and his title; and the Estates held at Tours under Charles VIII, his son, were well grounded in putting things back in their first state, and within the bounds of equity. The Kings who have followed, have kept themselves to a praiseworthy moderation. Louis XII deserved the name of Father of the People. Henry IV, nourished in the license of the wars, outside the discipline of the true Religion, attacked by arms, irritated by pens, discredited by a million invectives, after having finally attained the Royalty, behaved himself so legally that he never made a breach in any fundamental law of the State, and never coerced any company of Judicature, never even molested any individual of those who compose them, to the point that in order to get the

Edict of Nantes passed, he took pains to honor President Séguier with the embassy to Venice, to avoid his opposition. We know too that having let escape a remark which was a little harsh against President Harlay, he sent for him the next day and excused himself."

Rightly interpreted, the clause *car tel est nostre plaisir*, in the letters patent, is not evidence against this conclusion: "As for that imperious clause which it is the custom to place at the end of the ordinances and Royal letters, *Car tel est nostre bon plaisir*, this is a slight objection, but concerning which all the other peoples reproach us, as the mark of our slavery. But those who have the slightest familiarity with our formalities, know that these terms signify nothing else than *tale est placitum nostrum;* such is our Counsel (*Conseil*). It depends, afterward, on the Parlements or the other lesser Judges to examine the justice of such Letters and to verify them if they are found legitimate and reasonable. But to think that this word *car* is a causative, which breathes a character of authority into the letters, and takes the place of an ineluctable reason, is not at all reasonable; and the practice of the ordinary Jurisdictions is opposed to it, who refuse daily letters furnished and closed with this clause. And it is this *car* which might justly be abandoned to the Doctors of the Academy, not only as being useless, but also of pernicious consequence. But the first ordinance where we find it used, was that of Charles VIII, of the year 1485, by which he forbids habits of gold and silk to persons of lesser condition, and reserves them for the nobility. At the end of this ordinance he adds: *Car tel est nostre plaisir*. In truth one cannot say that the Kingdom of France can complain of such an edict; and it could be easily pardoned that King, if he had alleged no other reason. It is one of the confusions of our age that persons of no position dress themselves and furnish their houses as sumptuously as Princes, and leave them no mark of distinction. And luxury is not simply an error against propriety; it is the origin of all the public peculations and robberies."

The subordination of the state to justice is, then, according to reason and the law of the French kingdom. It is also Christian.

This appears in the passage which follows the one just quoted, which reads: "Let us return to this absolute power; and say that it is not compatible with our customs, whether Christian or French. There would be no more need of the State; there would be no more need of the Parlement; the consecration of our Kings would have to be abolished and the oath which they make on the Holy Gospels, to do justice, to prevent exactions, and to treat their subjects with equity and mercy: Those are the very terms of the formula of their oaths."

In France the Kingship was originally constituted and has continued to exist to the end of justice. But what is justice? To this author it is more than divine law and right reason: the King is also subject to the civil law: "Bodin," he says, "in his *République*, leg. 2, ch. 3, thinks he has said a lot, and believes it is great kindness on the part of Kings to submit to the laws of nature; as for the civil laws, he thinks that they are raised to a great height above them! It is in this chapter that he is so rash as to qualify as impertinence Aristotle's discourse on the division he makes of the different Royalties, in the fourteenth chapter of the third book of his *Politics*. But in this part, he is an indiscrete zealot, who has not remained unanswered. Cujas (who lived at the same time), with much less affectation, and much greater knowledge, has written a capital decision of this matter, in these terms: *Hodie Principes non sunt soluti legibus, quod est certissimum, quoniam iurunt in leges Patrias;* it is on the law 5 ff. de Iust. et Iure. The Pythagoras of the Gauls, the Seigneur de Pibrac, who had been advocate general of the Parlement, as eager for the honor of the King as equitable in the interest of the people, does not hesitate to say that he hates those words of absolute power."

Though limited by the law, and the people's right of resistance, the King is evidently free as regards other constituted authority. At the end of the pamphlet, it is true, the Parlements are called the defenders of the Prince and the people, and the Princes of the Blood are said to be "subject to no sovereign power except by duty of honor," but in a passage where the question of counsel is dealt with, the author refrains from saying that the King must act by advice. This is as follows: "No one of them (the philosophers) approves this unlimited power: one desires that there should be a Council composed of experienced persons; another that there should be a dominant law, of which the Prince is only the executor and the being. The empire of the law, says Aristotle, is something divine, permanent, and incorruptible; the absolute empire of man alone is brutal, because of covetousness, and the fury of the passions, to which Princes are subject, as much as, and more than, other men. Our adversaries object and say: if he who commands is regulated and circumscribed by the law, if he is attached to counsellors, he is no longer a King; he is only simple Magistrate. We reply that we do not dispute names or terms, but that we are working for the definition and the solid and legitimate establishment of the thing. What we call King in France, in Germany is an Emperor, in Moscovy a Duke, at Constantinople a Grand Seignior; but everywhere, of these Seigniors and these Kings, the people expect justice, protection, and comfort (*soulagement*). In some places Kings enjoy a full sovereignty; in others they are only feudatories; all are obliged to render justice. . . . There are as many formulae of government as different nations . . . but all these nations agree in this principle, that justice be administered to them. All the other qualities are accidents and circumstances."

2. DIVIDED AUTHORITY UNDER LAW. CLAUDE JOLY.

The writers treated in the preceding section, while affirming that the King is under law, and that resistance to his commands in certain cases is lawful, fail to declare that there exists in the state constituted authority independent of the King: to them, apparently, the kingdom of France is fully monarchical. But this group is a small minority in the body of defenders of the opposition; the majority held that in addition to the limitation of the law, the power of the King is restricted by that of other authorities: the kingdom of France is not fully monarchical. In this majority group is the great theorist of the Fronde, Claude Joly.

Of this writer's two important treatises on public law, the *Collection of Maxims* and the *Treatise on the Restitutions of the*

Great, the first is by far the more complete, and in expounding his doctrine we shall make use mainly of this book.

To Joly, as to almost all the writers on both sides of the controversy, the King is subject to divine law. He begins his argument in the *Maxims* by devoting a long passage to the refutation by exegesis of the great absolutist text, the passage in *Kings* where Samuel tells the Jews that the King will take their sons and daughters, etc.[8] Christianity is the rule of politics, and the base of public law, the fundamental law of the state. The following passage is in Chapter III, *On the office of a King in Religion:* "It is a very great error, which Kings ought to be warned against, to believe that Politics and Christian piety are incompatible, and that it is impossible to reconcile (*accomoder*) the laws of the State with those of the Gospel."[9] Kings, though elected by the people, are established by God: "Even though Kings hold their power originally from the people, that does not mean that they do not hold it also immediately from God, for one does not go against or prevent the other. As soon as the contract is made by which the people divest themselves of their power in favor of the Prince (*le peuple se démet de son pouvoir entre les mains du Prince*) and the Prince promises to do justice and to protect the People, God ratifies it and approves it, and gives it all the force necessary to be executed: and consequently the Prince draws all his authority from this divine approbation and virtue, which is as the seal of this synallagmatical act (*cet acte synallagmatique*)."[10]

Kings, then, are established by God to do justice. But what is justice? Joly insists that it is more than revealed truth and reason: it is also the civil law, the customs and ordinances of the kingdom: "Kings are established principally to do Justice; I do not think that it is difficult to prove, that they are likewise held to the Laws, since that which does not conform to approved and received Laws, cannot pass for just . . . our Ordinances . . . forbid the Judges to defer not only to *Lettres de Cachet*, but also

---

[8] Joly, *Maximes*, Chapter II.
[9] Joly, *Maximes*, 63.
[10] Joly, *Maximes*, 134-135.

to all which are contrary to established and received laws, and Declarations duly verified."[11] He appeals on this point to the authority of Seyssel: "Messire Claude de Seyssel, speaking particularly of the Kings of France, says openly in his *Monarchy* addressed to the King Francis I, who found nothing in it to criticize, that the Royal authority and power is regulated and controlled by three principal checks: that is to say by Religion, Justice, and Police, which is the Ordinances made by the Kings themselves and approved by the peoples."[12] He quotes Seyssel again on this point: "The King and Monarch, recognizing that by means of the Laws and Ordinances, and praiseworthy customs in France concerning Police, the Kingdom has attained the glory, grandeur, and power which is now seen, and keeps and maintains itself in peace, prosperity, and reputation, ought to keep them and cause them to be observed as much as he can, considering also that he is obligated to do so by the oath which he makes at his coronation."[13]

According to Joly, then, the King is limited by the laws of the Kingdom. But he goes farther, and maintains that the King is not the sole judge of the lawfulness of his acts. He quotes the *Inst. du Droit François* of G. Coquille on the authority of the Parlement in legislation: "One of the principal rights of the Majesty and Authority of the King is to make general Laws and Ordinances for the universal police of the Kingdom. But they are not really (*proprement*) Laws unless they have been received and approved according to (*avec*) the forms. For he adds immediately: The Laws and Ordinances of the Kings ought to be published and verified in the Parlement or other Sovereign court according to the nature of the subject (*selon le sujet de l'affaire*): otherwise the subjects are not bound by them. And when the Court adds to the act of publication that it has been by the express command of the King, it is a sign that the Court has not found the Edict reasonable."[14]

[11] Joly, *Maximes*, 149-150, 153.
[12] Joly, *Maximes*, 164.
[13] Joly, *Maximes*, 166-167.
[14] Joly, *Maximes*, 159-160.

Coquille, in the passage cited, while disapproving forced registration and implying that a law not freely registered is hardly binding, nevertheless refrains from giving the judges independent authority. Joly, however, has no doubts in this matter. He quotes Du Haillan's *Estat des affaires de France* as follows: "Although the State of France is a Monarchy, nevertheless by the institution of an infinity of fine political things, which render it flourishing, it seems that it is composed of three kinds (*façons*) of government: that is to say, of Monarchy, which is the government of one; of Aristocracy, which is the government of grave and wise personages; and of Democracy, that is to say, popular government. First it has the King, who is the Monarch loved, revered, feared, and obeyed; and though he has all power and authority to command and to do as he pleases, nevertheless this great and sovereign liberty is regulated, limited, and bridled by good Laws and Ordinances, and by the multitude and diversity of the Officers who are both near his person and established in divers places in his Kingdom: not everything being permitted him, but only what is just and reasonable, and prescribed by the Ordinances, and by the advice of his Council. So that it would be hardly possible for the Kings to do things too violent, or of too great prejudice to their Subjects, because they have about them several Princes, and other illustrious personages, who serve as axes, to cut off from their will what is superfluous and prejudicial to the public. . . . From that it comes that our Kings, having their power limited, are much more loved, honored, and feared by their subjects than are those whose power is without limits (*débordé*), without any moderation or rule."[15]

This idea, that the King shares public authority with other powers, Joly expresses forcibly in his own words in the following passage: "What our old writers (*anciens*) have left us and made us understand when they have said that *the King is always a minor*, is not that he may constantly break his contracts and promises, as their ill advised successors have interpreted it, but that it is a warning to him that he ought not administer anything without good and legitimate counsel: which is in conformity with

[15] Joly, *Maximes*, 167-169.

another law inviolably observed, by which the King cannot alienate five sols worth of his domain, all of which are things established for minors."[16] Among the propositions for which the *Maxims* were condemned by the government was the one at present being discussed, expressed by the King's attorney as follows: "That the French Monarchy is not purely monarchical, because of the power of the Estates and the Parlements." The *Letter of Apology* defends this proposition by alleging again the authority of Du Haillan, and that of Charles du Moulin, quoted as follows: *"Ergo solum caput non omnia potest; imo persona principi non est caput nisi organicum, sed verum caput est principatus ipse cum membris integrantibus eum."*[17]

Among the powers which share the authority of the state with the King, Joly would apparently put first the Estates General. In the eighth chapter of the *Maxims, Concerning the Estates*, he gives them an important share of the state. He begins, however, rather weakly, by expressing doubts in regard to the King's obligation to summon them. In the following quotation from De Thou, assembly of the Estates is put not on law but on policy: "In the general assemblies of the Estates, the subjects enter as in conference with the Prince, to whom they expose their complaints and grievances with a moderate liberty: as on the other hand the Prince causes his own to be heard by all the Orders of the Kingdom, which are sometimes more equitable than theirs: whence it happens that afterward they bear more willingly, more patiently, and without murmuring, keeping always the obedience which is due the Sovereign, not the yoke of the King, but the yoke of the Kingdom, oppressed by a quantity of burdens."[18] A little farther on he implies that the King may not be obliged to summon the Estates: "Those who say that the King diminishes his power (in calling the Estates) are in error (*ne le prennent bien*). For even if the King be not forced and obliged to take counsel of his people (*Car encore que le Roy ne soit contraint et necessité*

---

[16] Joly, *Maximes*, 171.

[17] *Lettre apologetique pour le Recueil de Maximes*, etc.

[18] Joly, *Maximes*, 269-270.

prendre conseil des siens), nevertheless it is good and proper that he do things by counsel."[19]

But Joly's real opinion is that under certain circumstances the King cannot refuse to assemble the Estates. This appears in the following passage: Louis XII did not call the Estates "not in order to gather to himself greater power, nor out of fear of giving authority to his people, or desire to treat them badly: for there never was a King more popular, or who loved the people more, so that after his death with great reason he was named Father of the people: but because he did not like to put burdens on his people, and when he was in need he found them very obedient, without assembling the Estates. Also he was careful to keep and preserve the persons and goods of his subjects, and provide for their necessities, without waiting to be requested to do so (*sans attendre qu'il en fust requis*)."[20] He quotes Du Haillan as saying that without the Estates France would be a tyranny: "Some have said that the Kings diminish their power in taking the advice and counsel of their Subjects, not being obligated or held to do so, saying that the Kings make themselves too familiar to them, which engenders contempt, and lowers the Royal dignity: but such people would like to make Tyrants of our Kings, who have found no other remedy for their affairs, when they have had need of money and aid, and our people no other remedy for their calamities than the convocation of the Estates, which has always been the sovereign medicine of the Kings and the people."[21] Joly also quotes an Italian, Davila, who says much the same thing: "the end of a legitimate and truly Royal government demands that the principal affairs be communicated to the general assembly of the Nation."[22]

It is already evident that Joly considered that the function of the Estates was to consent to taxation and to present complaints to the King. He conceived of this second capacity as one of reform, reëstablishment of the constitution. This is clear in the

---

[19] Joly, *Maximes*, 277.
[20] Joly, *Maximes*, 281.
[21] Joly, *Maximes*, 282.
[22] Joly, *Maximes*, 346.

following passage: The Estates which are about to meet should "reëstablish . . . with firmness and vigor our ancient Customs, Laws, and Ordinances: which is a power the Estates have, and will always have, because their power is of public right, and therefore imprescriptible."[23] Early in the book, when attacking the Concordat, which put the appointment of the Bishops in the hands of the King and the Pope, he urges that this matter be brought up in the coming Estates, and that the ancient form of election be reëstablished by them, "this being an affair for the Estates (*estant un ouvrage d'Estats*), and one of the most important that they could conclude and establish (*conclure et arrester*)."[24]

These two quotations imply that the Estates have power beyond that of petition. In fact Joly is convinced that the Estates possess, constitutionally, independent legislative authority. He says that if in recent years they have presented their requests to the King in the form of petitions, by him to be allowed, and then authorized by the Sovereign Courts, this is to be attributed to the love and respect of the French for their King: "For it is true that not only in the early times of our Monarchy, but also for long after, the Estates used a greater power, and even established and ordered (*et mesme de statuër et ordonner*)."[25]

And the Estates have at times exercised executive authority: an assembly of Estates in the reign of Charles VI called to account the financial administration. With this and other precedents in mind, Joly proposes that the coming Estates nominate commissioners to supervise the carrying out of the reforms ordered; the following passage occurs immediately after the one quoted above on the reform function of the Estates: "And in the second place they should provide for the execution of these (the ancient laws) by Commissioners and Deputies, which shall be appointed until the next Estates, which can be indicated at a briefer interval than in the past (*que l'on pourra indiquer à temps plus brief que par le passé*), who will keep an eye on the

[23] Joly, *Maximes*, 363.
[24] Joly, *Maximes*, 91.
[25] Joly, *Maximes*, 288.

maintenance of what has been resolved by common consent, as has been done formerly quite often in France."[26]

The other function of the Estates is consent to taxation. He insists that consent is required, quoting, like many other opposition writers, the famous passage from Commines: "Is there King or Lord on earth who has the power, beyond his domain, to put a denier on his subjects without the permission (*ottroy*) and consent of those who will pay, except by tyranny or violence? To which he replies as follows: No prince can do it otherwise (*ne le peut aultrement lever*) than by consent (*ottroy*) unless by tyranny, and he be excommunicated. But there are many stupid enough not to know what they can do and what they cannot in this matter."[27] In the *Maxims* Joly states that this consent belongs to the Estates, though in the *Restitutions* he says that it can be exercised by the Sovereign Courts, as the representatives of the Estates. This power dates from the first instance of taxation, in the reign of Philip the Fair: "When the Bourgeois had replied that they would willingly aid him, the King thanked them, which shows that Philip the Fair recognized that he did not himself have the power to tax his subjects (*imposer de luy-mesme sur ses Sujets*), and that this depended on the Estates."[28]

After that on the Estates General, Joly devotes a long chapter to the Parlement. He begins by defending the Court against the charge made by many supporters of the government, that their opposition was egotistical, as proved by the fact that they had not moved against the government until their wages were involved. This is not true, Joly says; if they have been slow to take action, it is because of the influence of certain leaders, the First President and others, who have been converted to absolutism; of these he says: "I shall say nothing to the prejudice of their honor, in accusing them of having desired to please the Court out of ambition or avarice, except that they have perhaps believed, following the new maxims of the time, that they were Officers of the King and not of the public, and that they owed more obedience

[26] Joly, *Maximes*, 363.
[27] Joly, *Maximes*, 334.
[28] Joly, *Maximes*, 316.

to the orders which bore the appearance of the Royalty than to what concerned the protection and relief of the peoples, overwhelmed under the mask of this pretended authority: although it is true that all the Royal Judges are no less Officers of the People than of the Prince: both contributing to their establishment by mutual correspondence: the Prince in nominating and presenting them to the people, that is to say, to the Companies which represent them, and the people in receiving and accepting them by the agency (*entremise*) of the same Companies."[29]

These new maxims, which have been responsible for the hesitation of the Parlement, were introduced by Richelieu, whose "government was as insupportable as his memory odious to posterity." Among them is the principle "that when the King has caused an edict to be published in his presence, it is not subject to revision, and ought to be executed without contradiction." This, says Joly, was denied by the Parlement as late as 1628. In that year the Court affirmed their right to pass on edicts registered at a *lit de justice*, declaring that "no Letters Patent or Declarations of the King should, by the Laws of the Kingdom, pass for verified, and are not obligatory, until they have been deliberated upon with liberty of suffrage by all the members of the Company, one after the other, and not by eight or ten, the first happened upon, whose opinions are taken as a matter of form by the Chancellor, making them vote by simply raising the hat (*les faisant opiner seulement du bonnet*)."[30]

The Parlement's power, then, in sanctioning royal legislation, is an independent one. Those who would deny it founding themselves on the *Car tel est nostre plaisir* of the edicts are in error: "It would seem," Joly says, "that these words were introduced and admitted in the Letters Patent in imitation of what was formerly put in the public acts of the things resolved in the ancient Parlements in these terms: *Quia tale est nostrum Placitum*, which meant nothing else than that what the act stated was the resolution which had been taken in the assembly: And by this same word, which had also many other meanings, the Parlement

---

[29] Joly, *Maximes*, 398-399.
[30] Joly, *Maximes*, 392-393.

was called."[31] He comes back to this matter in the *Letter of
Apology*, alleging the authority of Budé, who says that *placitum*
and *arrestum* are the same thing, and of Dr. Conanus.

The judges, possessing independent power, are constitutionally
irremovable. Joly appeals to the Ordinance of Louis XI and the
authority of Bodin: "Bodin, Book 4 of his *Republic*, Chap. 4,
toward the end, says that Louis XI . . . made an Ordinance by
which he declared all the Offices perpetual: and that those who
should be invested with them could not be deprived of them
except by resignation, death, or forfeiture: and by another edict
in explanation of the first (*declaratif du premier*), published and
verified the twentieth of September, 1482, it is declared that the
deprivation of the officers having forfeited shall not take place
unless the forfeiture is judged."[32] On this point he refers also to
Seyssel, Part I, Chap. 10. Partly with the intention, doubtless,
of insuring further the independence of the judges, Joly advocates
strongly, after an attack on venality, the reëstablishment of elections in the Parlement. The ancient rule for the filling of va-
cancies was for the King to choose one of three nominees of the
Court. The Estates of 1483 demanded that this rule be reëstablished, and it was so ordered by Charles VIII. The Estates of
Orleans made the same demand, which was granted by Charles
IX, who reënacted the ordinance of Charles VIII.

To Joly, then, the judges possess an important share of the
power of the state. His chapter on the Parlement contains, in
fact, one of the strongest statements of Parlementary authority
that I have found: "And so whatever certain persons say, who
find it strange that a Sovereign should be subject to the judgment
of his subjects, there is nothing in this which goes against reason.
For if it is true to say that Kings ought to render Justice to their
peoples, and that as a consequence of this indubitable maxim
they are subject to the Laws, as we have shown above, it is very
equitable that they should be under their Officers (*soubmis à leurs
Officiers*) in what concerns Justice and the Laws, and principally

[31] Joly, *Maximes*, 401-402.
[32] Joly, *Maximes*, 371-372.

in things which can harm others (*qui peuvent porter prejudice à autruy*)."[33]

Joly thought that the Parlement had power not only in legislation, but, as has already been said, in taxation.

Taxation was one of the great issues of the controversy. After having dealt twice with this subject, first in connection with divine law, second in the chapter on the Estates, he devotes a whole chapter to it, the eleventh, *That Kings have not the right to place imposts on their subjects without their consent.* This he begins by attacking the formula: Kings are masters of the lives and goods of their subjects. The word master, he says, should not be used: "When it is a question of expressing oneself in proper and significant terms, I say that the word Master is diametrically opposed to that of King. For the persons who are relatively opposed to the Master, as are slaves or even simple domestics, are, in this respect, made for the Master. But it is not at all true that subjects, who are relatively opposed to the King, are in this respect made for the King; on the contrary, as has been shown before, it is the King who in this respect is made for the subjects."[34] Private property is the law in France. Joly quotes a remonstrance of Jean Juvenal des Ursins to Charles VII: "Whatever some say of your ordinary power, you cannot take what is mine. What is mine is not yours. Very likely in Justice you are the Sovereign, and final appeal is to you (*va le ressort à vous*). You have your Domain, and every private person his."[35]

Since private property is the law, it can be taken only for the public good, and according to the forms: "Tailles cannot be imposed on the people except by urgent necessity or evident utility and by consent (*octroy*) of the people of the Estates."[36] This principle is enunciated as follows in the *Restitutions:* "Although the Prince has the power to impose new tailles on his free subjects for the utility of the public good, and when he cannot provide for these things from his own domain, he ought to do it according

[33] Joly, *Maximes,* 376.
[34] Joly, *Maximes,* 424.
[35] Joly, *Maximes,* 430.
[36] Joly, *Maximes,* 434.

to the laws and the ancient forms of his State, which are always unchangeable, and cannot be altered on the pretext of any necessity."[37]

In the passage above, the form for taxation is the grant of the Estates General. But in the *Restitutions* Joly says that consent can be given by the Sovereign Courts: "Since the Estates General, where this consent was given formerly are now assembled only rarely, the sovereign Courts, which represent them, now give it for them, when they judge it proper and necessary."[38] Their right in this matter is absolute: "If the verification of a bursal edict is made without liberty of suffrage, one can say that it is an act of violence, and the levy an extortion, since it is made in spite of those who should consent to it. And from this one should conclude that all imposts raised without these essential formalities are not due him who exacts them: and consequently he is obligated to restitution."

The forms should be observed, too, in the collection of taxes. The following passage is a fine expression of one of the major grievances of the time, and also contains a strong statement of the principle of consent: "To-day these courses and formalities of justice are thought too gentle and troublesome: it is quicker to send into the villages whole companies of Cavalry and Infantry, who live at discretion in the houses of the poor peasants, until they have paid enormous sums, which it is as impossible for them to find in their purses as to touch the sky with their finger, as the Jurisconsults say: so that they have to obligate themselves, and practically sell themselves, to get help from their friends to purchase freedom from the insufferable vexation which is inflicted upon them by these barbarous and inhuman people. And nevertheless all the Casuists who accord the sovereign Prince the power to impose subsidies on his subjects, do it on condition that the levy be made with moderation. . . . The true reason for this indulgence is, that the impost is a kind of gift, and as Commines says, a grant. But by civil law and natural equity, a donor should not be forced to execute his promise, *nisi in quantum*

[37] Joly, *Restitutions*, 39.
[38] Joly, *Restitutions*, 48.

facere potest. And that is why it is commonly said that the Cour des Aides is *the justice where are condemned those who owe nothing.*"[39]

Joly devotes the chapter in the *Maxims* after the one on taxation to another great issue of the time, relations with foreign countries. He quotes Seyssel on this subject as follows: "First I will make a maxim, that all Princes who have the government and handling of the State and Seignory, should love and seek peace with all neighbors and foreigners who are not by nature and diversity of Law enemies, as are the infidels, when they can hope this peace to be good, true, and entire, and one should move war against no one out of coveteousness of domain, human glory, or other disorderly passion."[40] This he follows with a quotation from Budé: "Christian Princes . . . cannot justly (*loisiblement*) hope for war, or undertake it for pleasure, unless against infidels and occupants of our boundaries: and with certain modifications, to augment or maintain the Catholic and Orthodox Faith, and uphold the honor and the name of Jesus Christ."[41] Joly approves of Grotius' suggestion to establish an arbiter of disputes between Christian states, and suggests the Pope: "To obviate the frequent misfortunes which come from so many wars which are made thoughtlessly between Christian Princes, he says that it would be not only useful, but also necessary that there should be a sovereign arbiter, by whose decisions the Princes would be forced to come to terms. . . . In this connection, if anyone could reasonably make himself the necessary arbiter between Catholic Princes, either to prevent them from undertaking war, or to bring it to a close, there is no doubt that this right would belong to the Pope as the common Father of Princes and People, who ought not allow his children to put one another to death. And if in this he should make use of the spiritual sword, that is to say, of excommunication, against those who were refractory to peace and reasonable composition, I believe he would do a thing agreeable to God."[42]

[39] Joly, *Restitutions*, 65-66.
[40] Joly, *Maximes*, 472-473.
[41] Joly, *Maximes*, 474-476.
[42] Joly, *Restitutions*, 76-77.

Joly ends the *Maxims* with the affirmation with which he began, that Christianity is the prime law of the state. The chapter
before the last is entitled *Of the three Royal virtues, Faith, Clem-
ency, and Liberality.* Here Mazarin is scathingly indicted for
asserting that he is not the "slave of his word," and for teaching
the King that "one who does not know how to feign and dis-
semble does not know how to reign." Such maxims, says Joly,
are Italian and Machiavellian. The last chapter is entitled, *That
God punishes more rigorously bad Kings than private persons.* This,
too, is the theme of the *Restitutions.* "If it is true," Joly says,
"that all men are responsible for the deed of another of which
they are the cause, one must not doubt that Sovereigns and the
Great are much more reprehensible and punishable before God
than others."[43]

[43] Joly, *Restitutions*, 18.

CHAPTER VI

DEFENSE OF THE OPPOSITION (II)

1. AUTHORITY OF THE PARLEMENT, OF THE PRINCES, OF THE ESTATES

To CLAUDE JOLY, civil authority in France is divided between the King, the Estates General, the Parlement, and the official Council, Princes and Officers of the Crown. The majority of the apologists of the opposition, like him, take the stand that the King is not alone in the government of the state; but they dwell more than he does on the authority of the Parlement of Paris or that of the Princes. This is, of course, what one would expect: we saw in the first chapters that the great issues of the conflict were the authority of the Parlement of Paris and of the Princes. In this section we will deal first with the defense of the Parlement, then with that of the Princes, and finally with the Estates General, which played a comparatively unimportant part in the polemic, as it did in fact.

Though they are concerned mainly with the question of authority, the subordination of the King to the law is affirmed by many of these writers, and implied by the rest. The author of the *Lettre d'Avis*,[1] the most famous opposition pamphlet of the first year of the Fronde, proves by the coronation oath that the King is subject to the laws of God, of reason, and of the kingdom. He says: "When the Kings come to the crown, they swear on the holy Gospels that they will maintain the Church of God to their best ability; that they will observe the fundamental laws of the State, and that they will protect their subjects according to God and reason, as good Kings should do; and in consideration of this oath, the people are obligated to obey them as Gods on

[1] *Lettre d'avis à messieurs du Parlement de Paris*, etc.

earth; and the oath to do so which they swore to the first Kings
still endures, because of the perpetual succession which is maintained in France. Both oaths are respective; and just as the King
can cause subjects to be punished severely who have broken the
promise which they have made to obey him as their legitimate
Monarch, in all matters not contrary to the three fundamental
articles which I have stated; so subjects are exempt from obedience, when Kings violate their oath; for if they overturn the laws
of the Church, who is the subject who will obey them, and who
is obligated to obey them? That is the great question, in fact,
of the time of Henry IV, to which he could find a solution only
by making himself a Catholic. If they break the fundamental
laws of the State, if, for example, they pretend to cause the
Kingdom to fall to the distaff, to sell or alienate their domain,
the subjects are not bound to give them another, or to obey
them on the other point. All this is without difficulty; and one
must conclude that it is the same for the third circumstance of
the oath, that if the Kings do not protect their subjects according
to right and reason, in conformity with the laws of God and the
Ordinances of the Estates which the sovereign Courts are bound
to cause to be executed, having them in trust, the subjects are
exempt from obedience; and even more, if they are oppressed
unjustly, and with tyrannical violence, which cannot be reconciled with Royal Monarchy, in which the subjects obligate themselves to the Kings only to be protected against those who might
trouble their repose; so that, if they trouble it themselves, they
cease to be Kings, and the subjects to be subjects."

The King is here held to observe the "Ordinances of the
Estates." Most of these writers are less specific and assert that
he is bound by the laws of the kingdom. In the *Observations on
the Sentiments of a Faithful Subject of the King*,[2] this obligation
is founded, as above, on the coronation oath. "The King's sovereignty," this author says, "consists particularly in maintain-
ing and observing them (the laws of the kingdom); that is his
oath, it is the first act of his Royalty, it is the most considerable
action of his Consecration, and the most solemn contract that he

[2] *Observations veritables et dés-intéressées*, etc.

makes with his people." Like Joly, this author appeals on this point to the authority of Seyssel: "After having shown that the authority and power of the King is regulated and limited by three checks, which are Religion, Justice, and Police; speaking of the last he (Seyssel) says that the third check which our Kings have is that of the Police, that is to say, of several Ordinances which have been made by the Kings themselves, and then afterward confirmed and approved from time to time, which tend to the conservation of the Kingdom in general and in particular, and which have been kept for so long that the Princes do not attempt to disobey them (*d'y deroger*) and if they attempted to do it their command would not be obeyed."

In the *Veritable Maxims of the Government of France*,[3] which was the great opposition pamphlet of 1652, the subordination of the King to the law is again strongly affirmed: "The sovereignty of our Kings is to do Justice, to do good of all kinds. They are the veritable Images of the Divinity, who can never do evil. Their sovereignty is absolute when it is a question of executing the Law, and not to destroy it." Like several other opposition writers, this author quotes Pybrac's quatrain:

> "Je hay ces mots de puissance absoluë
> De plein pouvoir, de propre mouvement:
> Aux saincts Decrets ils ont premierement
> Puis à nos Lois la puissance toluë."

"Our laws," says Pybrac: the civil law, then, has imperative force. The last sentence of the *Veritable Maxims* reads: "As for me I will obey only the King and the Laws of my country, which are two inseparable things."

Subject to the law, the King is also, according to these writers, subject to counsel. The last pamphlet quoted contains the following passage on this point: "The person of the King is the body of the royalty, it is always holy and sacred. It is for this reason that it is accompanied by a number of Officers, Guards, and Nobility, and that stately vestments have been invented with which the King is clothed in the great ceremonies, to inspire

---

[3] *Les véritables maximes du gouvernement de la France*, etc.

respect and veneration in the minds of the peoples. But the soul of the Royalty is quite a different thing. It is the Law, it is Justice, it is the public orders, it is the order of the government, it is the ancient custom, which our Moderns have badly called the Salic law, which admits only males to the government, and which has always excluded all women. It is the general Police of the Kingdom which requires that everything be done by the concert of the King and the peoples conjointly." This "concert" is achieved in the Parlement: "The moment that it is a question of something in which the people have an interest; it is not in the Council that it should be resolved: the King can contract with his people only in his Parlement, nor can he destroy anything that he has done except in the same place: it is a contentious matter (*matière contentieuse*)."

The authority of the Court is independent: the author of the *Veritable Maxims* cites the Ordinance of Louis XI: "This Prince speaking of his Officers says: That they are essential parts of the state (*la chose publique*), and members of the body, of which he is the head." The independence of the Parlement is affirmed strongly in the *Observations on the Sentiments of a Faithful Subject of the King*. One passage in this pamphlet reads: "To qualify their Sovereign authority by the expression *subaltern Power* is to render oneself ridiculous, and even more, since all France is dependent on them (*releve d'eux*), and they on nobody, being the only Judges of their own confreres; while they are recognized as the sole and sovereign Judges of the suits and differences which arise between the King and his subjects, of the verification, rejection, and modification of his royal commands (*voluntez*), Edicts, and Ordinances." In another place this author says that the Parlements, and especially that of Paris have an independent (*non participé*) authority according to the fundamental Laws of the Monarchy, and in another, that "the authority which is called in law: *Imperium* belongs to them and to none other than these ancient and natural Counsellors of the Sovereign." This pamphlet also contains a refutation of the absolutist argument founded on the clause, *Car tel est nostre plaisir*. "There is no need," it reads, "to sound so loud the authority of a King who is major before the age of fourteen, to maintain that there are no other limits and no other laws than his will, as he shows in his Edicts and his Patents which are concluded and end always with these words of a Sovereign: *Car tel est nostre plaisir.* We know that this clause is there, and that these words can be read there, but we also are not ignorant of the fact that it is after having made an ample deduction of the causes and the motives which have led him to make this Ordinance, and after mention has been made of the Princes and great personages whose advice he has made use of in resolving it, and causing it to be observed as a Law: Beside the fact that all these pompous clauses and these ostentatious words have no force and no effect until after the Parlement has verified and registered them. A great Magistrate[4] of our day has not hesitated to say and pronounce in one of his learned and generous Harangues of the year 1648 in the presence of His Royal Highness: that our Kings had kept these words *Car tel est nostre plaisir* in their Edicts only to render their domination more venerable and more mysterious, and not to disobey reason and take counsel of no one."

The independence of the Parlement is affirmed strongly also in the *Lettre d'Avis.* "Remember, then, Gentlemen, (the author is addressing the Court) that you are those Consenting Gods (*Dieux Consentes*), without whom the Kings can do nothing just or of consequence in the government of their peoples; that you should be the asylum and the guardian Genii of all France, the Light of good morals, and the Masters of Equity." The expression *Dieux consentes* occurs in several other pamphlets. Some express the same idea with the phrase *tutors of the Kings*, and in a great many the Parlement of Paris is compared with the Roman Senate.

The Parlement's authority is, then, independent. It is also very extensive. In a passage quoted above from the *Veritable Maxims*, "all matters in which the people have an interest" must be settled by agreement between the King and the Court. In another passage in the same pamphlet the Parlement's power is

[4] There is a note in the pamphlet at this place which says that this person was Nicolaï, First President of the Chambre des Comptes.

more explicitly defined to include taxation, the creation of new offices and new titles, treaties with foreign countries, the appointment of regents, etc. To the King and his Council are left only minor matters of administration: he can there treat of recompenses; "it is proper also to deliberate there (when war has been decided upon) on whether or not to give battle." The *Observations on the Sentiments of a Faithful Subject of the King* has the following passages on the jurisdiction of the Court. "It is an authority," this author says, "which has no limits except those of the Royalty, since it constitutes the throne of our Kings, keeps their bed of Justice, and is the source and principle of all the other Sovereign and subaltern authorities of the Kingdom, who can do nothing and execute nothing unless it come from its orders, from its commands (*mandemens*), and from its necessary and indispensable verifications." The Parlement is "the Council where war is declared, where the treaties of peace are confirmed, where the Regencies are authorized, where the majorities of the Kings are declared, where the Laws and Ordinances of the Kingdom receive their force and their vigor, and where the Royal authority rests as in its source with such brilliance and such splendor that there is no one who does not receive it and recognize it when it has passed there, and not otherwise." He quotes a Parlementary remonstrance to Louis XIII, of the year 1615: "Charles V, uniting justice and the Royal power, never declared war, and treated of no important affair, except by the advice of his Parlement, and he who had acquired in all the nations the lofty title of Wise, was proud (*faisoit gloire*) of having withdrawn one of his Provinces from a foreign hand by a decree of his Parlement."

One of the most important of the rights of the Parlement is that of sanctioning taxation. It will have been noticed that this figures in the list of the Court's powers given in the *Veritable Maxims*. It is also affirmed in the *Lettre d'Avis*. I will quote this pamphlet at some length, for it is the best statement on the subject of taxation that I have found outside Joly.

The author begins by denying the proposition that the King is master of lives and goods; the passage has already been quoted in part: "These detestable thieves have tried for the past thirty years to get us to accept a Tyrannical Politics and published everywhere that the King has the right of life and death over his subjects, that our lives and our goods are his, and that he can dispose of them as he pleases, being the Sovereign Master. It is true that subjects are naturally obligated to employ their lives and their goods for the service of their Prince; but there is great difference between these two propositions: the Prince can take and dispose of our lives and our goods according to his fancy; and we should employ lives and goods for the Prince. The first supposes a despotic and seignorial power; and the second a subjugation in the subject which obligates him to serve his Prince at the expense of his blood and his goods, when the need is great. Never has France been a despotic government, unless in the last thirty years when we have been subject to the Mercy of Ministers and exposed to their tyranny. Those who philosophize only on present things, and do not bring their minds to seek truth, believing that it is enough to be imbued with an *Everybody says so*, will be astonished perhaps by this proposition; but let them learn that France is a pure Royal Monarchy, in which the Prince is bound to conform to the laws of God, and in which his people, obeying his, remain in natural liberty and property in their goods; while the Despotic governs subjects as a father of a family his slaves. Such is the government of the Turk, who for this reason is called the Grand Seignior, who can without injustice command his *Bassas* to bring him their heads, having made himself master by arms, and having always retained the power of Conqueror, which gives, according to the law of nations (*le droit des gens*), the power to treat as slaves those whom one has subjugated." France, however, has never been conquered, and is free: "it being a thing unheard of to say that a leader who is submitted to voluntarily, has the same right over those who yield themselves, as a Master or Lord over his slaves."

In a royal monarchy like France the King can take nothing beyond his domain except by consent of the subjects: "One should distinguish carefully between Tribute taken generally and the quality of the Tribute. There is no subject who does not owe, in his quality of subject, some tribute to his prince, which is nothing else, properly considered, than a subsistence given him for the maintenance of his house and for the affairs which concern the security and repose of the State. And this is what we call Domain; with this the Kings of the first and second race, and even many of the third, contented themselves, without raising anything more from their subjects, unless in some extraordinary case.[5] It should be noticed that this Domain is inalienable, because the subjects affected it at the beginning to the subsistence of the Kings, and because they obligated themselves to pay these revenues by natural law; so that whoever does not do it, besides mortally offending God, is bound to make restitution, because they have abandoned it (*ils s'en sont dessaisis*) in favor of the subsistence of the Prince. But it should be noted that they have never given up cognizance of the extraordinary subsidies which it has been necessary to raise from them, and there is no prescription which can acquire for the Kings the right to make levies without their consent, for any cause whatsoever. The reason for this is drawn from the maxim which we have stated: that the King has no right over the goods of individuals; and therefore he cannot force them to give them to him without injustice." Louis XI was the first to break this law, and Commines remonstrated to the Estates held under his successor that no Prince had a right to do it.

This author holds that the consent of the people to extraordinary taxation should be given in the Estates General or the Parlement. This is clear in the note quoted above, and in another passage, which reads: "Before Louis XI, the Kings raised nothing from their subjects except by consent of the Estates, or at least which was not authorized by the court of Parlement." The Taille is extraordinary revenue, and therefore subject to consent: "The tailles, which today mount to such excessive sums, are not due him (the King) according to the laws of the Kingdom, and

---

[5] The author has the following note at this place: "When I speak of the peoples, I do not mean individuals (*les particuliers*); but the Estates and the Parlements which represent the people (*qui sont pour le peuple*)."

the Kings his predecessors never raised them except by violence or tolerance."

The works which have been examined thus far in this section have been centered in the defense of the Parlement. The Fronde also brought forth, as we have indicated, a considerable body of writings in defense of the authority of the Princes. Most of these appeared, of course, in the second phase of the controversy.

They claim for the Princes an important portion of public authority, usually associating them with the Officers of the Crown or the Parlement. The *Discourse to the Parlement on the detention of the Princes*[6] contains the following passage: "You, Gentlemen (the Parlement), . . . are the Protectors of the Laws and of innocence, the sacred guardians of the Royal authority, the sole Judges of the Princes of the Blood, who are with you the principal Columns of the Monarchy." In the *Visible Decadence of the Royalty*,[7] as in this first pamphlet, the Princes are associated with the Parlement. The kingdom of France, this author says, is partially aristocratic: "The French State does not condemn the Aristocratic, but it subordinates it to the Monarchical: if this latter attempted to be independent to the point of being unwilling to defer in anything to the Aristocratic, that is to say to the guidance of those nearest the Crown, and of the wisest established by their participation; it would be despotic or tyrannical, and consequently should be got rid of. . . . The King can do nothing without counsel: this counsel should be composed only of his Princes or those who are called to it by their participation."

The most famous of the works in defense of the Princes, the *Union of the Princes*,[8] associates them with the great lords and the Officers of the Crown. "We promise," this pamphlet reads, "to employ unanimously all our power, our lives and our goods . . . to put the State back in its first form, to establish under the sovereign authority of the King the legitimate Counsel of the Princes of the Blood, of the other Princes and Officers of

[6] *Discours au parlement sur la détention des princes.*

[7] *La décadence visible de la royauté*, etc.

[8] *L'Union ou Association des Princes*, etc.

the Crown, and of the old counsellors of State who have passed through the great offices, and of those who are extracted from the great Houses and ancient families, who by natural affectation and personal interest are inclined to the conservation of the State."

Extreme claims for the Princes are advanced in the *Royal au Mazarin.*[9] Their right to a share of the government is a matter of fundamental law: "The participation of the Princes of the Blood in the government of the State has passed into fundamental law, which the Sovereigns cannot to-day disturb without giving just cause for all sorts of troubles."

Though the male relatives of the King were usually grouped together, there was a tendency to distinguish between the immediate family of the King and his more distant relatives: the term Princes of the Blood was frequently reserved for the latter, while the former were called Children of the King, or Sons of France. One writer goes so far as to deny all authority to the Princes of the Blood, implying at the same time that the son of a King possesses a great deal. This is the author of the *Discourse on the deputation of the Parlement to the Prince of Condé.*[10] The passage is as follows: "For besides the fact that there is no instance in the registers of the Parlement's ever having made on such an occasion like compliments to the Princes of the Blood, who are subjects of the King as well as we, who are subject to the same laws which bind us, and have no other advantage than to be the first Gentlemen of the Kingdom, it was impossible also to cite as precedent the Deputation which had been made to the Duke of Orleans, who being a son of France, Uncle of the King, and Lieutenant General of the Crown, is raised infinitely above a Prince of the Blood and merits therefore special honors; and the Parlement, doubtless, gravely offended his Royal Highness in making him the equal of a man who speaks to him only with his hat in his hand."

The explanation of the authority of the Princes is implied in the phrase above, from the *Union of the Princes:* "natural affec-

[9] *Le Royal au Mazarin,* etc.
[10] *Discours sur la députation du parlement,* etc.

tion and personal interest." The *Request of the Three Estates* [11] has the same idea in the following passage: "And in order that France, and the Kings, Princes, and peoples may not again fall into a like servitude (the rule of a minister) let the Princes give themselves the trouble, as children of the House, and their interest bound with those of the state, while those of French favorites are always contrary, to tend these affairs with their own hands." The interest of the Princes is, of course, that they or their descendants may succeed to the Crown. This is stated in the *Letter of Nacar to Rivière*.[12] This writer says that Orleans should have a care for the State "to which he and his descendants can pretend."

In the writings of the Fronde defenses of the Estates General are, as we have said, comparatively rare. We have seen, however, that the greatest of the apologists of the Fronde wrote at length on this subject. There are also a few pamphlets, most of them of the year 1651, when occurred the Assembly of the Nobility.

These writers in general take a very high tone. The author of another *Request of the Three Estates* [13] says that a decision of the Estates binds the King. One of the passages where this appears is as follows: "Thus everybody admits, as much as all good Frenchmen desire it, that Mazarin will infallibly receive the coup de grâce in the Assembly of the Estates General, and that the good destinies of France have reserved this occasion to allow no further grounds to fear his return, when Justice pronouncing her oracles by the mouth of all the demigods of the Monarchy will make ring a sentence against this outlaw from which there is no appeal, not only discrediting him in the Annals, but making it impossible for the sovereigns to reëstablish him without violating the fundamental Laws of this State." In another place in this pamphlet the Estates General are called the abridgment of the Monarchy, and the author says that the "passions of the peoples would be entirely complaisant to all their judgments."

---

[11] *Requeste des trois états présentée à messieurs du Parlement.*
[12] *Lettre du sieur de Nacar à l'abbé de la Rivière,* etc.
[13] *La Requeste des trois estats touchant le lieu et les personnes,* etc.

The more common doctrine, that decisions of the Estates must be sanctioned by the King, is set forth in the *Request of the Nobility*:[14] "Your Majesty will permit us," this author says, "if it pleases him, to say to him that it is time to work at all these things (reform of the Kingdom) and that we believe that it would be impossible to succeed more effectively than by this Assembly. Since it would be more famous and more authentic than any other, we believe that it will find more veneration and deference in the minds of the peoples; that the Ordinances which will emanate from the absolute power of Your Majesty on the petitions (*cayers*) which are presented to him, will be followed by a purely voluntary observance, and that Your Majesty, imitating in this circumstance the prudence of his predecessors, will not derive from it lesser advantages than they have in less extreme necessities."

It seems to have been generally believed that the Estates General held the first place among the secondary authorities of the state. Claude Joly was evidently of this opinion. It appears in certain government pamphlets, which attempted to discredit the Parlement by opposing the authority of the Estates to that of the Court. One of these, the *Request of the Peoples of France*,[15] has the following passage: "The Parlements are neither the total nor the principal. They have place only in the Third (Estate). That of Paris, by its circular letters, confesses that the others ought at least to be associated with them, since they share with them a same authority. They are ten brothers of the same father and mother, who are the King and France, who never die. The elder son, because he has a larger portion, does not entirely exclude the cadets. But if they were all assembled in a single body, their authority would be always borrowed and limited; it would be always subject to that of the King; it would be always relative to that of the Estates General; it would be at most only a Third; Our Lords themselves do not deny that the Clergy and the Nobility are the first parts."

The defenders of the Parlement in general confessed the supe-

[14] *Requeste de la noblesse*, etc.
[15] *Requête des peuples de France*, etc.

riority or at least the equality of the Estates: we shall show in the last section of this chapter that it was generally held that the Court derived its power from the Estates. There were some, however, who gave a superior position to the Parlement. This was affirmed, we have seen, by a member of the Court. Sandricourt,[16] in a pamphlet in defense of the Estates, says that the Parlement is not above them, "though they boast that they can modify the Resolutions of the Estates General."[17]

The theory that the constitution of France is one of divided authority would appear to offer the opposition a solution of the problem of obedience: an authority which is independent must protect itself against coercion. This, however, I have not seen anywhere distinctly affirmed, except possibly in the following passage from the *Lettre d'Avis*,[18] and here it seems that the Parlement orders resistance not as a power independent in its sphere, but as the supreme authority of the state. The author, addressing the Parlement, says: "You know better than I that the peoples have no deliberative voice . . . except by you who are as their deputies; and when I said that they are sometimes exempt from obedience I did not mean that private persons could assume this right; otherwise they would do themselves justice according to their caprice, which cannot be; but only when they are authorized by your Decrees, which are equivalent to Estates and ordinances (*qui tiennent lieu d'Estats et d'ordannances*). Remember then, I beg you, that since the sedentary parlements were instituted to render justice more completely to the subjects of the King, the Estates have been held only to remedy the disorders which occur from time to time in the administration; that they have been given the Ordinances as in trust, to cause them to be executed in their form and tenor, and that they are charged with this duty both by the Sovereign and the Subjects; so that one can conclude in conformity with my proposition, that all the corruption which occurs in the State comes only from the cowardly tolerance of the Parlements, and that the people and the

---

[16] For Sandricourt see C. Moreau, *Bibliographie des Mazarinades*, I, 7-13.

[17] *Les Préparatifs de la descente du cardinal Mazarin aux enfers*, etc.

[18] *Lettre d'avis à messieurs du Parlement de Paris*, etc.

Kings can demand an account from them for a justice so badly administered."

2. THE MINORITY

The literature of the Fronde shows that the minority was generally looked upon as a quasi interregnum. Opposition writers of all shades of opinion asserted that the power of a Regent was inferior to that of the King; the silence of the government apologists on this point would indicate that they found it impossible to deny this contention.

It was commonly said that the Regent was more strictly bound by the law than the King. One of the champions of the Princes says, speaking of their arrest, "this detention is contrary to the forms and the laws of the Kingdom, which in time of minority ought to be observed, without a Regent's being able, by virtue of her power, to deviate from them or to violate them."[19] In the *Theologian of State to the Queen*[20] this idea is expressed as follows: "It is well known that Regents of the Kingdom, male and female, are not the Originals of authority, but the Guardians (*Depositaires*), and that if they attempt action beyond the ancient orders of the Kingdom, one can oppose the Law without offending them."

A number of opposition writers declared that the Regent was incapable of changing the law. The following verses are from the *Burlesque Request of the Partisans:*[21]

> "Mais pourtant c'est un a scavoir
> Si Régente avoit le pouvoir
> De fulminer des bulles telles
> A ses bons suiets mortelles,
> Car c'est en purs termes de droit
> Tout ce que le maieur pourroit,
> Ne tenant lieu que de tutrice
> Et de simple administratrice

[19] *Factum pour Messieurs les Princes.*
[20] *Le Théologien d'Etat à la reyne.*
[21] *Requeste burlesque des partisans au Parlement.*

Qui ne peut rien sans nullité
Changer durant minorité."

The *partisans* are here supposed to allege this rule against the establishment of the Chamber of Justice ordered by the Declaration of July 16th, 1648. The same doctrine is set forth in a passage in the *Moral and Christian Maxims:*[22] "Regents . . . are in an order extremely inferior to that of the Royal dignity; all that they are owed in this quality, is only the deference which a servitor should render him who is the guardian of his master. That is why I shall remark in passing upon the indiscrete zeal, or, to speak better, the ignorant zeal of certain persons who, at the beginning of the Regency, caused to be added in the prayer for the King, after the words *Pro rege nostro Ludovico*, these others: *Et pro Anna Regina nostra;* for the Kingdom of France does not fall to the distaff; and its Sovereignty is not divisible into two parts with equal power. Thence it comes that Regents, male and female, or all their Council, Ministers and Favorites, not being sovereign, cannot during their Regency and the minority of the Kings, make any change or establishment which has force of Law; for the power to make Laws is an effect of the absolute authority which resides in the sole person of the Prince, and is incommunicable to any person whomsoever; so that the Regents, being only guardians, properly speaking, have only the right to conserve, and not to destroy, change, or innovate; so consequently they cannot make any Laws or Ordinances, or create any new Offices, which are all functions of an independent and major King. And there is reason for astonishment that the Sovereign Courts have tolerated creations of Offices during the minority of the King, which he can abolish without wronging anybody, when he attains his majority; for it is to play the sovereign and to encroach upon the authority which is inseparable from his person to put new Officers in his State."

The Regent, then, is incapable of legislation, and especially of alterations in the structure of the state. Some writers allow such acts, but insist that they must be sanctioned by other au-

[22] *Maximes morales et chrestiennes*, etc.

thorities. This appears in a passage in the *Summary of the Curious Doctrine of Cardinal Mazarin*.[23] The Cardinal is supposed to be put the following question: "If, abusing the authority of the Regency, and extending its power farther than it should go by the fundamental laws of the Kingdom, I have not exercised my ministry as if I were administering the State under a major King, promising cities in sovereignty to Monsieur le Prince, causing to be created all kinds of Offices, and other like acts, which depend upon the full power of the King, which cannot be exercised by anyone whomsoever, unless on some urgent occasion, in the ordinary forms, that is to say, with the approbation of the Estates or of the Parlement which represents them?" Mazarin replies: "I have never made any difference between the authority of the King, exercised by himself, as a major, and that which is confided to a Regent during his minority, and I am quite certain that those who make so much noise over this difference which they have imagined, could not show me the basis for it."

This writer would subject the important acts of the Regent to the sanction of the Estates or the Parlement. There are some who maintain that all acts of the Regent must be approved. In this group are several of the champions of the Princes. One wrote: "As for entrance to the Council during the minority, it cannot be considered a favor to a Prince of the Blood, who has a fundamental right to it by birth and by the condition of the time."[24] The same idea is expressed in another pamphlet as follows: "If all the fundamental laws of the State were well observed, the Princes of the Blood would be otherwise considered in the Council of the King, since they are the legitimate administrators of the state during the minorities of our Kings."[25]

If these last writers thought that the Princes had powers in the state under a major King, they evidently considered them greater during a minority. Many of the group whom we considered in the last section, who held that public authority in France was divided, declare that in a Regency a greater share of power

23 *Sommaire de la doctrine curieuse du cardinal Mazarin*, etc.
24 *Factum pour Messieurs les Princes.*
25 *Lettre d'un marguiller de Paris*, etc.

devolves upon the secondary authorities than normally. This is implied in the *Lettre d'Avis* [26] and in the *Observations on the Sentiments of a Faithful Subject*.[27] Another pamphlet, the *Reasons or Veritable Motives of the Defense of the Parlement*,[28] after showing that the Parlement has an important share of public authority, declares that the Court "during the minority is the veritable Tutor of the Kings and the sacred Guardian (*Depositaire*) of the Crown; it is responsible for it to the King and to the Public." This idea is clear in the following sentence, from the *Justification of the Parlement*:[29] "The Parlement is the natural tutor of our Kings, principally during the time of their minority."

The reason for the inferiority of a Regent to the King is implied in the words "administrator," "tutor," "guardian," which have occurred in most of the passages quoted. The King can be trusted with greater power because the welfare of the state is his own, just as a mature person can be trusted to administer his estate. A Regent, however, has not the same motive of self-interest; the powers of a Regent, therefore, must be limited, as are those of the guardian of a minor.

The absence of the motive of self-interest, then, weakens the authority of a Regent. But in the Fronde the Regent was a woman, and in the opinion of some, the authority of the government was further impaired by a presumption of the inferiority of women. In the *Blindness of France since the Minority*[30] the Salic law is said to rest upon this base, and is extended to include Regents. The passage is as follows: "The Salic Law should teach them that the French sceptre does not spin, and that provision makes it fall to the distaff as well as inheritance . . . holy Scripture should have taught them that man being the head of woman, they could not give absolute command to a woman, without violating the design of Providence, which created her only for servitude."

[26] *Lettre d'avis à messieurs du Parlement de Paris*, etc.
[27] *Observations veritables et dés-intéressées*, etc.
[28] *Les Raisons ou les motifs véritables de la déffense du Parlement*, etc.
[29] *La Iustification du Parlement et de la ville de Paris*, etc.
[30] *Aveuglement de la France depuis la minorité*.

The majority of the Kings of France at the age of fourteen was a political fiction: Le Bret, it will be remembered, had to resort to mysticism to justify it. We saw that in the second part of the Fronde there was a project to extend the minority to the age of twenty-one. This was advocated in a number of writings. The following passage is from the *Observations on the Sentiments of a Faithful Subject*,[31] written after the majority. "Our history, and the Registers of the Parlement show that young Kings like ours, whom may God preserve, are accustomed to come to the Parlement with the Princes of the Blood, there to choose and ask for Ministers and faithful Counsellors to govern the State; and the Princes of the Blood, being Ministers born and natural governors of the Kingdom, having a right to the Crown, cannot be excluded from the council, to give the first place to an ignorant foreigner, against the Laws of France."

For a number of the apologists of the opposition the theory of the quasi interregnum offered a solution of the problem of obedience. The following passage is from the *Letter of the Chevalier Georges*:[32] "This is not the extravagant tumult of an insolent populace; it is a necessary armament, authorized by those who are the depositaries of the authority of the King in his minority, against the enemy of his State, and for ancient liberty."

3. THE MINISTÉRIAT

The great mass of opposition pamphlets are attacks on the minister, as indicated by the name *Mazarinades* which has been given to the whole body of writings connected with the Fronde. Most of these are of no direct value to us, consisting of invectives against Mazarin. There are some, however, which found their attacks upon the constitutional principles which we have seen affirmed in the official declarations.

The legality of the *ministériat* is denied in the *Veritable Maxims*.[33] The author, addressing the Duke of Orleans, says: "You have at last recognized, Monseigneur, how fatal to the

---

[31] *Observations veritables et dés-intéressées*, etc.
[32] *Lettre du chevalier Georges de Paris*, etc.
[33] *Les véritables maximes du gouvernement de la France*, etc.

state has been this newly invented name of Minister, this bastard authority." The same stand is taken in the *Request of the Three Estates*,[34] the most famous of the pamphlets against Mazarin. The passage reads: "Although since the death of Louis XIII, of happy memory, the Princes, great Lords, and Officers, remembering the enormous injustices and intolerable evils done to them and the whole Kingdom by those who have seized upon the absolute power near the King under the new name of first minister of State, had protested loudly that they would never again suffer a private person to raise himself thus upon the shoulders of the King and to the oppression of everybody, nevertheless, by their too great kindness it has happened that a foreigner named Iulle Mazarin has installed himself in this sovereign ministry."

It will be remembered that the argument against the *ministériat* in the remonstrance of the Parlement of January 21st, 1649 is that the minister cannot have that will to the good of the kingdom which is the King's. The *Request of the Three Estates* declares that the interest of favorites is always contrary to that of the state. Mazarin has bled France white: "He has pillaged and ravished all the Finances of the King and reduced his Majesty to extreme indigence, and all his subjects to poverty worse than death; for not only has he exhausted all there was of ready money by *comptants* amounting to fifty and sixty millions a year; but also he has consumed in advance three years of the King's revenue, so as to confuse and entangle forever the order of the finances; he has strangely authorized and increased that cursed race of Partisans who, come for the most part from lackeys and grooms, have all France under the whip, have farmed the tailles, and caused them to be raised by companies of fusiliers who are so many unchained Demons, have created a great quantity of officers of all kinds, and made daily insufferable impositions, for the execution of which they have employed cruelty and tortures capable of drawing the marrow from the bones of the unhappy French, who would have been glad to be quit in abandoning to them all their property and eating grass like poor beasts, there having been seen 23,000 prisoners at a

---

[34] *Requeste des trois estats présentée à messieurs du Parlement*, etc.

time in the Provinces of the Kingdom for the taxes of the Tailles
and other imposts, of whom 5,000 died in this languor in the
year 1646, as can be verified by the entries and registers of the
Jailors." Much of the money thus raised was not used in the
service of the state, but taken by the minister: "He has not paid
the soldiers nor the pensions, though he charges large sums to
these accounts to cover his robberies, nor provided the frontier
fortresses with men and munitions, nor paid what was due the
Navy and the Artillery, whose appropriations are more than four
years in arrears; he has done nothing to assist persons of virtue
and merit, nor given any recompense to those who have squan-
dered their property and their blood in the service of the King;
on the contrary he has caused to perish of hunger and need
almost all the armies of the King, which, having received in the
past five years only two installments of pay a year, more than
120,000 soldiers have died of destitution, need, and horrible poverty; so that it is certain, and can be proved by several irreproach-
able witnesses, that he has divided large sums of money with
those whom he has placed in power, and has himself swallowed
up the greater part, which he has had transported as well by bills
of exchange as in coin and precious stones, and this under the
pretext of making war in Italy and conquering certain fortresses
like Piombino and Portolongone." This writer, like many others,
accuses Mazarin of protracting the war in order to continue his
depredations.

Another argument against the *ministériat*, brought forward
in a number of pamphlets, is that the minister, being a usurper,
is bound to rule tyrannically. It is stated in the following passage: "We have never seen the Kings illtreat their blood so
frequently as when they have abandoned the helm of the State
to some favorite. If the great of the Kingdom do not submit
slavishly to his dishonest commands, he thinks that they envy
him his fortune, and treats them as enemies."[35] Many writers
ascribe the destruction of the ancient constitution to the rule of
ministers, which some begin with Richelieu, others with the
Maréchal d'Ancre.

[35] *Lettre du chevalier Georges de Paris*, etc.

It was shown in Chapter III that officially the opposition denied the legality of the *ministériat* only once, during the blockade of Paris; their other attacks on Mazarin were founded on the law which excluded foreigners from the Council. This second ground is the one taken in most of the works which deal with this subject.

The explanation of this law given by the Advocate General was that the foreign minister could not be trusted to prefer the King's interests to those of his other master. The same thing is said in many pamphlets; Mazarin was born in a country of Spanish allegiance, and is accused of betraying France in the war with Spain. Another, very common, argument was that the foreign minister, being prejudiced against the customs of the state, or ignorant of them, is bound to pervert them. It is stated as follows in the *Reasons of state against a foreign minister*:[36] "The foreign Prince (says one of our Doctors) desiring to make the people conform to the habits and customs of his own country, and believing that what is proper there, is, and ought to be, in the State where he commands, not only will not correct it, but will cause its ruin. And so the thing for which the Emperor Probus was praised most highly was that he knew the natures of all the nations of which his Empire was composed. That is why the best of our Historians says that even if a Stranger should govern the State well, nevertheless because of the difference between his mind and ours, his way of living, and that of the French, he will always give some cause for complaint, it being impossible for him to know accurately the Republic which he governs, as natural Subjects do, this knowledge being absolutely necessary to him above all things."

The illegality of the *ministériat*, or of a foreigner's holding the position of minister, furnished the opposition with an easy solution of the problem of obedience: a government dominated by a foreign minister possessed no lawful authority, and could be resisted. This stand was taken, it will be remembered, by the Parlement in the remonstrances of January 21st, 1649. The idea is expressed in the following passage from the *Moral and Chris-*

---

[36] *Raisons d'estat contre le ministre estranger.*

tian Maxims:[37] "This obedience and respect (which is owed the King) is not due the council of Ministers and Favorites; for it is a theology unknown to Antiquity, which has been put forward in the last few years by the artifices of the late Cardinal de Richelieu, to declare crimes of high treason the faults committed against Favorites and Ministers called of state. We do not find this maxim in the Gospel, no Council has established it; none of the Fathers has taught it."

But more than this, it is a duty to oppose the minister. He has usurped the King's power; the King's subjects are obligated to restore it to him. The consent of the King to the usurpation is of no moment, since he cannot abdicate his authority. If he has given it, he has acted under coercion, he is the "prisoner" of the minister. The Parlement, it will be remembered, in July, 1652, made the Duke of Orleans Lieutenant General "in order to free the King from the captivity in which he was held by Cardinal Mazarin." This idea is expressed in a passage in the pamphlet last quoted: "And since the person of Kings is the most precious and sacred thing that people can have, after those of Religion, there is nothing which they are not obligated to do and undertake to preserve them in the security of their life, in the sovereign liberty of their independence, to prevent their being carried away or led into captivity, and to draw them from it if by any chance they have fallen into it. This maxim needs no proof. . . . There is, then, greater obligation and duty to unite and take arms to oppose the abduction of so sacred a person, or to withdraw it from this violence which is a pure captivity, than there is for the defense of all which can be imagined below it."

4. THEORY OF CONSTITUTIONALISM

It was shown in the last section of Chapter IV that the government's argument rested mainly upon "reason." It has already appeared in our examination of the official declarations that the argument of the opposition rested upon the law.

The works written in defense of the opposition confirm the

---

[37] *Maximes morales et chrestiennes,* etc.

official statements. On reading them it becomes clear that the Fronde, to the members of the party, was a movement in defense of the constitution of the kingdom.

The great reform of the year 1648 was not new law, but old, the reëstablishment of the ancient form of the kingdom. Statements like the following arc very common: "The Parlement, being unable to suffer longer the disorders of the Ministry, which were about to destroy the ancient government and the Principles of the French Monarchy, has succeeded by its care and credit in obtaining from the King that famous Declaration of the month of October 1648, which serves as a barrier to the violence of the Ministry and restores the ancient Laws in their vigour."[38]

The corruption of the constitution is recent. To the writer just quoted it dates from Richelieu, as to most of those who deal with this subject, including, as we have seen, Claude Joly. In the *Summary of the Curious Doctrine of Cardinal Mazarin*,[39] the minister makes the following reply to the question why he had violated the Declaration of October 22nd: "Because experience has made it clear to the Queen and her council that to maintain this Declaration it would be necessary to overthrow the maxims by which the great Cardinal de Richelieu had begun so happily to govern the Kingdom, and which I have since abetted by the fine instructions which he gave me, and which I am proud to hold of such a great Politician; which Her Majesty and her council have not judged proper to do; since it would mean allowing the authority of the King to return from the high point to which we have raised it, to that with which the earlier Kings contented themselves with great inconvenience, subject as they were to the formalities of the Estates and assemblies of their peoples for things of consequence, in which nevertheless the absolute authority of the King shines forth much better than in common and daily affairs." The Fronde, according to its apologists, was an attempt to restore the constitution of the state, which had been recently subverted.

To the opposition writers, then, the constitution of the king-

---

[38] *Advis important et nécessaire, aux corps de Ville*, etc.
[39] *Sommaire de la doctrine curieuse du cardinal Mazarin*, etc.

dom is binding. But why? Whence did it derive its binding
force? In most of these works this question is unanswered: the
authors are content with pointing to the law. There is a considerable number, however, in which solution of this fundamental
problem is attempted.

Many base the constitution upon an original contract between
the King and the people. The Kingship, they say, was a creation
of the people, who had originally lived without a King. They
had then established one, but for their own convenience, and on
their own terms. The act of creation of the Kingship was a
contract: the people surrendered their liberty to the King in
consideration of certain specified services. But since the succession of Kings has been uninterrupted from the beginning, the
present King's power is the same as that of the first King: it is
still a conditional grant of the people. The King is still bound
by his original contract; he is responsible to the people for the
services which are the conditions on which he holds his power.
All this appears in a passage already quoted from the *Reasonable
complaint against the last Declaration of the King:*[40] "Of whatever
date is the origin of a Monarchy, it cannot prescribe the liberty
of the nation which has given it being and beginning. It is a
maxim indubitable in Law, and which lawyers (*les gens de robbe*)
ought not to be ignorant of, that *nemo potest sibi mutare causam
possessionis.* Hugh Capet was elected by the estates of France
to reign equitably and according to the laws of the country; he
made a solemn oath to do it at the time of his consecration; he
consequently transmitted the Kingdom to his posterity on the
same condition. If Louis XI attempted things beyond this, he
sinned against his duty and his title."

This author was a member of the group who held that except
for his subordination to the law the King was unlimited; the
original contract, to him, then, on the King's side, was no more
than the maintenance of the law. Many of those who held that
the King was also limited by the authority of the secondary
powers of the state found this limitation, as well as his subordination to the law, upon the original contract: the people sur-

[40] *Le raisonnable plaintif sur la dernière déclaration du Roy.*

rendered their liberty to the King on condition that he maintain the law, and also that he act by the advice of a council. This is expressed in the following two passages from the *Royal au Mazarin*.[41] "The power of our Kings is only a voluntary award (*deference*) of the liberty of the subjects, who renounce their natural right to be subject to nobody, to receive the yoke of a sovereign whom they commit unanimously to the maintenance of their laws." But, "since the intention of the peoples, who of their own free will have subjected themselves to the authority of a Monarch, has never been to allow them a despotic power, that is to say, a power independent of any kind of counsel, the nearest (to the King) and the wisest among them have been appointed to fill this place, and to govern the management of the affairs of State conjointly with the sovereign, though dependent upon him."

The council established by the original contract exists at present in the Parlement, the Princes, and the Estates. Identification of the Parlement with the primitive council especially demanded apology. It was attempted in the *Royal au Mazarin* as follows: "We have already dwelt at too great length on the birth of the Parlement of Paris, which, being nothing other than a continuation, not once interrupted in eleven centuries, of that ancient Assembly which the Francs held in the Champ de Mars to deliberate on the affairs of State, and which was given the name Parlement under Philip the Fair, and which was placed in the Palace of the Kings under Louis le Hutin, is consequently to-day in the same authority which it had then; and since its resolutions were then Sovereign in matters of State, can one reasonably say that they are less independent, since the Parlement is nothing other than a continuation of that ancient Assembly of the French which has never been interrupted?" Claude Joly has a like explanation; he says: "From the Estates General of France the Parlement derived its origin, and as when it was ambulatory it was the equivalent of these Estates (*à l'instar de ces Estats*), after it was made sedentary it remained, as Du Haillan says, with the same functions and prerogatives that it had when it

---

[41] *Le Royal au Mazarin*, etc.

followed the Kings. Thence it comes that it has the right, and the other sovereign Companies which have been drawn from it or erected in imitation of it, to verify all edicts, bursal and others: that is to say, to see, examine, receive, moderate, or refuse them, as they judge best."[42]

But the Parlement was a body of judges, mainly occupied with administering the law. How could a governmental assembly like the Champ de Mars or the ancient curia have become a court of law? The answer is as follows in the *Veritable Maxims:*[43] "Louis Hutin gave it his Palace. And at the same time public business not presenting itself every day, it began to take cognizance by appeal of the important and weighty cases which concerned only individuals. The Parlement did not for this reason lose cognizance of public affairs. It took good care not to renounce so advantageous a right; it still represented that general assembly of the Francs. If it had become sedentary, it still kept its dignity and its power." The *Royal au Mazarin* offers the same explanation, and concludes: "And so power both in public and private affairs was given it: but with this difference, nevertheless, that this latter is accidental, and the former essential, for it was established in the first intention only to deliberate on public matters."

In the *Veritable Maxims* the present composition of the Parlement is pointed to as evidence of its origin in the ancient Council. The passage reads: "In fact we see that the Parlement has always been an abridgment of the Three Estates. Still to-day we see the Church represented there by a number of clerical Counsellors, there we see the Nobility in the persons of the Princes of the Blood, and the Dukes and Peers of France, who are the first of the Crown. Finally the entire body, which is a mixed body, represents all the Orders of the Kingdom. The King has there his bed of justice, following the example of that August Tribunal, upon which he was always raised in the general Assembly of the French at the beginning of the Monarchy, or in the Assembly of

---

[42] Joly, *Restitutions,* 46-47.
[43] *Les véritables maximes du gouvernement de la France,* etc.

the Grandees of the State under the second Race, and for more
than three hundred years under the third."

The Parlement had, in fact, until recent times, exercised the
functions of a supreme council. In the *Veritable Maxims* there is
a long recitation of outstanding examples of the Court's participation in public affairs. The Parlement had established Regents,
had sanctioned taxes, had ratified treaties.

According to these writers, the constitution of the Kingdom
rests upon a contract. What does this mean? Evidently that
public authority is looked upon as a form of property. The King
possesses his authority (we saw the word used above), but no
more than his authority, no more than his "title" warrants. If
he takes more, if he governs by his will rather than the law, or
usurps the authority of the secondary powers of the state, he
violates the terms of his grant, and invades the property of another. That other is the people, with whom he has contracted
for his authority. The property which he would be taking would
be the people's property in their liberty; part of this liberty they
have given to the King, the remainder, however, belongs to them.
The contract theory seems to rest finally upon the property right
of the people in their liberty.

The sanction of the contract theory is the principle of the
sanctity of property. But those who found the constitution upon
a contract, also, almost invariably, appeal to nature, or reason.
We have already seen that in the *Royal au Mazarin* the liberty
of the people is a natural right. If it is their property, it should
be their property; freedom is in accordance with the law of nature. In the *Veritable Maxims* also, liberty is called natural.
Referring to the primitive assembly of the nation, the author
says: "Everybody took part in the deliberation, because our
Monarchy had been founded on liberty; there never was a government more natural." Another statement of this idea in the
same pamphlet reads: "But what is remarkable in our government is that it is quite natural, that is to say that everything has
always been done by the consent of the Sovereign with his subjects and of the subjects with the Sovereign." The *Reasonable
complaint against the last Declaration of the King* rests upon reason

as well as the contract: Polybius, Aristotle, Cicero, this writer says, all assert that people have elected Kings to do them justice and to protect them; and if they had not said it, he continues, "can it enter common sense that they could have done otherwise?"

In the last pamphlet Scripture is appealed to as well as reason, and the constitution is declared to be Christian. There are many other like statements. In the *Lettre d'Avis*[44] the royal monarchy, that is, monarchy subject to the law and counsel, is "according to the maxims of Christianity." Claude Joly may have meant the same thing by his *synallagmatical act*. I repeat the passage: "Even though Kings hold their power originally from the people, that does not mean that they do not hold it also immediately from God, for one does not go against or prevent the other. As soon as the contract is made by which the people divest themselves of their power in favor of the Prince, and the Prince promises to do justice and to protect the People, God ratifies it and approves it, and gives it all the force necessary to be executed: and consequently the Prince draws all his authority from this divine approbation and virtue, which is as the seal of this synallagmatical act."[45] God is the Christian God, known through revelation; the teaching of the Church, then, is the source of the law of the state. This seems to appear in other passages in Joly's works, among them the following: "It is a very great error, which Kings should be warned against, to believe that Politics and Christian piety are incompatible, and that it is impossible to reconcile the laws of the State with those of the Gospel."[46]

But Joly's idea was probably different. It will be remembered that quoting Seyssel he subordinates the government to justice as well as to religion. But justice is reason, and reason, as well as revelation, was looked upon as divine. Revelation did not abrogate reason, but supplemented it. An act founded on reason would, then, be compatible with Gospel. And reason must frequently be appealed to, for on many matters God is silent. Joly

[44] *Lettre d'avis à messieurs du Parlement de Paris*, etc.
[45] Joly, *Maximes*, 134-135.
[46] Joly, *Maximes*, 63.

may have considered that the organization of the state is among these; when he says that God has approved the constitution he may not have meant that the principles of the constitution are contained in the doctrine of the Church, but that the constitution is just: God wills justice.

If the constitution, then, rests upon the people's right in their liberty, it also rests upon reason, and God's will. The government which the people created is good, and divine. This act of creation was an award of justice; the people were the representatives of God, the channel of His will. But if the test of the constitution is justice, the source of the law is a matter of no importance. In the *Observations on the Sentiments of a Faithful Subject*[47] it is said that the Parlement may have derived their authority from the King, but this act was good, and the King is bound by it. The passage is as follows: "The Parlements . . . and especially that of Paris, have an independent authority according to the fundamental Laws of the Monarchy; whether because it has an establishment as old as that of the Royalty, and occupies the place of the Council of the Princes and Barons who since earliest times were near the person of the Kings, as born with the State; whether, finally, the Sovereigns have confided to it as in trust the care and conservation of the Laws, to which they have been willing to subject themselves, following the example of God, who in the conduct of the Universe, according to the thought of a Father of the Church, commanded once to obey always, as we see Him firm and constant in the execution of His word, which changes never." The King of France is subject to the laws; being so, it is just that he be subject to the counsel of the guardians of the laws, those whose office it is to know them.

According to this second supposition, the constitution is a rational means to secure the enforcement of the law. The Parlement's authority rests not upon their quality of representatives of the people, but upon their guardianship of the law. But if they have no voice in government, the people are still free: true freedom is subordination to the law. This last writer quotes de Thou as saying: "Give back their authority to the Laws and to

[47] *Observations veritables et dés-intéressées*, etc.

your Parlements, holding for certain that towns and cities have soul, life, and movement only by the Laws, and are unable, just as bodies would be without souls, to use their members, their strength, and their blood, unless they obey the Laws: But Judges and Magistrates are the Ministers and interpreters of the Laws, of which we ought all to be serfs, in order all to be free."

BIBLIOGRAPHY

BIBLIOGRAPHY

I. FOR CHAPTERS I AND II

It was my original intention to draw my account of events from the authorities, Lavisse, Chéruel, Bazin, and Sainte-Aulaire, but I soon discovered that this would be impossible: they contradict one another, and leave many of my questions unanswered. I was obliged to go to the sources. To these I found the best guide to be M. Henri Courteault in his edition of the Journal of Vallier. I have drawn extensively upon Chéruel's and Bazin's work: the former for the motives of the government, and for the movements in the provinces; the latter for the movements in the provinces and for assistance in the establishment of dates.

The works made use of for the first two chapters are as follows:

Aubery, A. L'Histoire du Cardinal Mazarin, 1688, 2 vols.

Aumale, duc d'. Histoire des princes de Condé pendant les XVIe et XVIIe siecles, 1863–96, 7 vols.

Barente, baron de. Le Parlement et la Fronde, 1859.

Bazin, A. Histoire de France sous le Ministère du Cardinal Mazarin, 1842, 2 Vols.

Boulenger, M. Mazarin Soutien de l'État, 1929.

Cans, A. Le rôle politique de l'Assemblée du clergé pendant la Fronde (1650-1651), Revue historique, CXIV, 1-60 (1913).

Chéruel, A. Les Carnets de Mazarin pendant la Fronde, Revue historique, IV, 103-138 (1877).

Chéruel, A. Histoire de France Pendant la Minorité de Louis XIV, 1879-1880, 4 Vols.

Chéruel, A. Histoire de France sous le Ministère de Mazarin (1651-1661), 1882, 3 Vols.

Courteault, H. La Fronde à Paris, 1930.

Fayard, E. Aperçu historique sur le Parlement de Paris, 1878, 2 Vols.

Feillet, A. La Misère au temps de la Fronde et Saint Vincent de Paul, 1868.

Glasson, E. Le Parlement de Paris. Son rôle politique depuis le règne de Charles VII jusqu'à la Révolution, 1901, 2 Vols.

Lavisse, E. Histoire de France depuis les origines jusqu'à la Révolution Publiée avec la collaboration de MM. Bayet, Bloch, etc., Volume VII, Part I, 1906. This volume is by Lavisse.

Mailfait, H. Un magistrat de l'ancien régime: Omer Talon, sa vie et ses oeuvres, 1902.

Mailly, J. B. L'Esprit de la Fronde, ou Histoire politique et militaire des troubles de France pendant la minorité de Louis XIV, 1772-73, 5 Vols.

Madelin, L. La Fronde, 1931.

Sainte-Aulaire, comte de. Histoire de la Fronde, New Edition, 1843, 2 Vols.

*   *   *   *   *

Debats du Parlement de Paris Pendant la Minorité de Louis XIV ou
  Memoires de ce qui se passa dans les assemblées du Parlement par un
  Conseiller qui entra en charge au commencement de la minorité, et
  assista à toutes ces assemblées. This is a folio manuscript, at the
  Archives Nationales No. U. 336. 600 pages.
Dubuisson-Aubenay. Journal, edited by Saige, 1883-85, 2 Vols.
Goulas, Nicolas, Mémoires, edited by Constant, 1879-82, 3 Vols.
Histoire (l') du Temps, ou le Veritable Recit de ce qui s'est passé dans le
  Parlement depuis le mois d'Aoust 1647 iusques au mois de Novembre
  1648. Avec les Harangues et les Advis differends, qui ont esté proposez
  dans les affaires qu'on y a solemnellement traittées, 1649, 336 pages.
Iournal de l'assemblée de la noblesse tenuë à Paris, en l'Année mil six cens
  cinquante-un [1651,] 199 pages.
Joly, Guy. Mémoires, in Series III, Vol. II of the Nouvelle Collection des
  Mémoires pour servir à l'Histoire de France, edited by Michaud and
  Poujoulat, 1838.
Journal du Parlement. I used the following editions of the Journal:
  Journal contenant tout ce qui s'est fait et passé en la Cour de Parlement
    de Paris, toutes les Chambres Assemblées, sur le suiet des affaires du
    temps present, Paris, Gervais Alliot et Jacques Langlois, 1648, 158
    pages.
  Suite du Journal contenant ce qui s'est passé depuis le premier de Febvrier
    1649, 54 pages, numbered 49 to 103.
  Suite du Journal de ce qui s'est passé au Parlement les Chambres assem-
    blées, jusques à la Paix, pages numbered irregularly from 325 to 427.
  These three works are bound in one volume at the Bibliothèque Mazarine,
    No. M. 12033.
  Suitte du Vray Journal des Assemblees du Parlement; Contenant ce qui
    s'est fait depuis la Saint Martin mil six cens quarante-neuf, iusques à
    Pasques 1651, Paris, Gervais Alliot et Jacques Langlois, 1651, 172
    pages.
  Suitte du Iournal des Assemblées du Parlement depuis la Saint Martin
    1650, iusques à Pasques 1651, 76 pages.
  These two works are bound together at the Bibliothèque Mazarine, No.
    M. 12038.
  Le Iournal ou Histoire du Temps Present: Contenant toutes les Declara-
    tions du Roy verifiées en Parlement, et tous les Arrests rendus, les
    Chambres assemblées, pour les affaires publiques. Depuis le mois
    d'Avril 1651 iusques en Juin 1652, Paris, Gervais Alliot et Jacques
    Langlois, 1652, 323 pages. At the Bibliothèque Mazarine this is No.
    M. 12011.
  Relation contenant la suitte et conclusion du Iournal de tout ce qui s'est
    passe au Parlement, pour les affaires publiques. Depuis Pasques 1652
    iusques en Ianvier 1653, Paris, Gervais Alliot et Jacques Langlois,
    1653, 263 pages. At the Bibliothèque Mazarine, No. M. 12012.

The Journal of the Parlement is strictly chronological, and my references can be easily found at the dates.

La Rochefoucauld, duc de. Oeuvres, edited by Gilbert and Gourdault, 1868-83, 3 Vols.

Lenet, Pierre. Mémoires, in Series III, Vol. II of the Nouvelle Collection des Mémoires pour servir à l'Histoire de France, edited by Michaud and Poujoulat, 1838.

Mazarin, Lettres à la reine, etc., edited by Ravenel, 1836.

Mazarin, Lettres pendant son ministère, edited by Chéruel, 1872-1906, 9 Vols.

Molé, Mathieu. Mémoires, edited by Champollion-Figeac, 1855-57, 4 Vols.

Montpensier, Mlle. de. Mémoires, edited by Chéruel, 1858-1868, 4 Vols.

Motteville, Mme. de. Mémoires, edited by Riaux, 1869, 4 Vols.

Ormesson, O. L. d'. Journal, edited by Chéruel, 1860, 2 Vols.

Registres de l'Hôtel de Ville de Paris Pendant la Fronde, edited by Le Roux de Lincy and Douet-D'arcq, 1846, 3 Vols.

Retz, Cardinal de. Oeuvres, edited by Feillet, 1870-96, 10 Vols.

Talon, Omer. Mémoires, in Series III, Vol. VI of the Nouvelle Collection des Mémoires pour servir à l'Histoire de France, edited by Michaud and Poujoulat, 1839.

Vallier, Jean. Journal, edited by Courteault and de Vaissière, 1902-18, 4 Vols.

II. FOR CHAPTER III

Isambert's Recueil Général des Anciennes Lois Françaises is incomplete and not entirely trustworthy. I have used it only when I had other evidence. The sources for this chapter are the Journal of the Parlement, the Memoirs of Talon, the Debats du Parlement de Paris (U. 336), and the following work:

Recueil de toutes les déclarations du roy rendues pour la police, Iustice et Finances de son Royaume énoncées en la dernière du mois de Mars 1649, insérée au présent Recueil et donnée pour faire cesser les mouvemens et restablir le repos et la tranquillité publique. Toutes lesquelles Déclarations Sa Majesté veut estre executées selon leur forme et teneur. Avec tous les Arrests de vérification et modification d'icelles tant du Parlement, Chambre des Comptes que Cour des Aydes, ensemble autres Déclarations des Roys Louis XI et Henry III, avec les Articles des Ordonnances de Blois et d'Orléans pour l'éclaircissement des Articles XIII, XIV et XV mentionnez en la Déclaration du 22 octobre 1648. Et encore une Table desdites Déclarations avec un Abrégé de ce qui y est contenu. *Paris*, par les Imprimeurs et Libraires ordinaires du Roy, 1649, 44 plus 16 pages and an index.

III. FOR CHAPTER IV

The literature of the Fronde is enormous: C. Moreau's *Bibliographie des Mazarinades* contains more than four thousand titles and is by no means complete (for supplements see Bourgeois and André *Les Sources de l'Histoire de France, XVIIᵉ siècle*, IV, 291-293). My method of acquainting myself with it was the following: I first read the extensive collection in Widener Library and C. Moreau's two volumes of selections (*Choix de Mazarinades*), and then went through the *Bibliographie des Mazarinades*, which is full enough to be an excellent guide, and marked the important works. I found them all at the Bibliothèque Mazarine, in Paris.

Very little has been done with this material, though I found the following works of assistance:

Brissaud, J. Un libéral au XVIIe siècle, Claude Joly, 1898.

Denis, M. J. Littérature Politique de la Fronde, 1892.

Lacour-Gayet, G. L'Éducation Politique de Louis XIV, 1898.

Lemaire, A. Les Lois Fondamentales de la Monarchie Française d'après les Théoriciens de l'Ancien Régime, 1907.

Sée, H. Les Idées Politiques en France au XVIIe siècle, 1923.

The works in defense of the government are comparatively few, and incomplete. I have supplemented them with the great work of Le Bret, and an earlier book of Naudé's:

Le Bret, C. De la Souveraineté du Roy, Paris, 1632, Jacques Quesnel, 709 pages, plus 4 pages of Choses obmises and an index.

Naudé, G. Considerations Politiques sur les Coups d'Estat, Rome, 1639, 222 pages.

The following is a list of the works in defense of the government which I found significant enough to note:

A qui aime la vérité, [1649,] 4 pages.

Anti-requeste (l') civille, 1649, 8 pages.

Bandeau (le) levé de dessus les yeux des Parisiens pour bien juger des Mouvemens présans et de la partie qu'eux et tous les bons François y doivent tenir, [Saint-Germain, 1649,] 12 pages.

Caractère (le) du royaliste à Agathon, [Paris,] 1652, 38 pages.

Changement (le) d'Estat sur la Majorité du Roy. Presenté à sa maiesté avant son Auguste Sacre et Couronnement, 1651, 11 pages.

Considerations des-interessees sur la conduite du Cardinal Mazarin, Paris, 1652, 32 pages.

Discours et considerations Politiques et Morales sur la Prison des Princes de Conde, Conty, et Duc de Longueville. Par M. L., Paris, Sebastien Martin, 1650, 31 pages.

Fidele (le) Politique, Paris, 1649, 15 pages.

Image (l') du souverain, ou L'Illustre portraict des divinitez mortelles, où il est traité de la dignité Royale, de l'ancienne institution des Roys, par qui est-ce qu'ils ont esté eleus, à quelle fin Dieu les a creez, iusques où se peut estendre le légitime pouuoir qu'ils ont sur nous, s'il est permis aux Sujets de iuger des actions de leur Prince, et de quelle reuerence il nous faut user en parlant de leur personne, contre l'opinion des Libertins du siècle, dédié à Sa Majesté, par P. B. E. *Rex verò laetabitur in Deo; laudabuntur omnes qui iurant in eo; quia obstructum est os loquentium iniqua.* Psal., 62, Paris, 1649, 24 pages.

Iugement et censure des trois libelles intitulez: la *Replique*, le *Donjon* et le *Rétorquement du foudre de Iupinet*, faits par l'Hypocrite à la fausse barbe. Iudas avois obtenu portion à l'administration des Apostres. Act., chap I, vers. 18, Paris, 1649, 35 pages.

Lettre ou Exhortation d'un Particulier a Monsieur Le Mareschal de Turenne Pour l'obliger à mettre bas les armes, Paris, Sebastien Martin, 1650, 39 pages.

Lis et fais, [1649,] 4 pages.

Lumières pour l'histoire de ce temps, ou Réfutation de tous les libelles et discours faits contre l'authorité royale durant les Troubles à Paris, avec les motifs de la stabilité et durée de la Paix contre l'opinion du vulgaire. *Fiat pax in virtute tua et abuntia in turribus tuis.* Ps. 121, Paris, 1649, 16 pages.

Pièce de Pontoise. Les sentimens divers sur l'arrest du Parlement du vingtiesme iuillet. Et le discours seditieux qu'on pretend faussement avoir esté fait par Monsieur Bignon, le 26. sur la Lieutenance du Royaume, 1652, 15 pages.

Question, si la voix du peuple est la voix de Dieu? 1649, 34 pages.

Réflexions chrestiennes, morales et politiques de l'hermite du Mont Valérien sur toutes les pièces volentes de ce temps, ou Iugement critique donné contre ce nombre infiny de libelles diffamatoires qui ont esté faits depuis le commencement des Troubles iusques à présent par des personnes. *Quid detur tibi, aut quid apponatur tibi ad linguam dolosam?* Psalm. 119, Paris, 1649, 14 pages.

Remontrance au Peuple par L. S. D. N. D. S. C. E. T., 1649, 24 pages.

Réponse à la *Résolution politique des deux principaux doutes qui occupent les esprits du temps,* scavoir est: Pourquoy est-ce que le Cardinal Mazarin a fait emprisonner Messieurs les Princes dans le temps de la Minorité, Et pourquoy est-ce qu'il s'opiniastre à leur détention en veuë des désordres qui troublent l'Estat, pour procurer leur eslargissement, dédiée à tous ceux qui voudront voir des raisons sans passion, des iustifications sans ambiguité, et des conclusions sans fallace, [1650,] 20 pages.

Responce et Refutation du Discours intitulé Lettre d'Avis a MM. du Parlement de Paris, par un Provincial, Paris, 1649, 31 pages.

Response au *Réveille-matin de la Fronde Royalle sur la honteuse paix de Bourdeaux,* 1650, 16 pages.

Response chrestienne et politique Aux Opinions Erronées du Temps. *Sancta Brigida: quando sedebit puer in sede Lilij, lunc dissipabit omne malum intuitu suo,* 1652, 14 pages.

Response (la) du père Favre, prédicateur et confesseur de la Reyne, sur la Harangue à elle faicte par un Reuerend Père Chartreux pour la Paix, Paris, 1652, 8 pages.

Requeste des peuples de France, Affligez des Presens troubles, à nosseigneurs de la Cour de Parlement, Scéant à Paris, 1652, 20 pages.

Roi (le) veut que le Parlement sorte de Paris, etc., 7 pages.

Sentimens (les) d'un fidelle suiet du Roy sur l'arrest du Parlement du vingt-neufiesme Décembre 1651, 1652, 73 pages.

Traitté de l'ancienne dignité royale et de l'institution des Roys, 20 pages.

Très-humble remontrance Faite à Monsieur le Prince de Condé, sur les affaires présentes, 1652, 15 pages.

Véritable (le) bandeau de Thémis, ou la Justice bandée, *Vae vobis qui iudicatis terram*, 1649, 11 pages.

Véritable censure de la *Lettre d'avis escrite par un provincial à messieurs du Parlement*, et la véritable censure de la Réponse à la mesme Lettre, avec la Refutation de la Replique à ladite Réponse, ou la Critique des trois plus fameux Libelles que nous ayons veu paroistre, depuis le commencement de ces derniers Troubles iusques à présent, Par un des plus Illustres Grammairiens de Samothrace. *Domine, libera animam meam à labiis iniquis et à lingua dolosa*, Psalm. 119, Paris, 1649, 24 pages.

IV. FOR CHAPTERS V AND VI

The works of criticism of the defense of the opposition are those listed at the beginning of Section III.

The great theorist of the Fronde was Claude Joly; his two important works (the *Codicille d'Or* is of little value) are the following:

Joly, Claude. Recueil de Maximes Veritables et importantes pour L'institution du Roy. Contre la fausse et pernicieuse Politique du Cardinal Mazarin, pretendu Sur-Intendant de l'education de sa Majesté avec Deux Lettres Apologetiques pour ledit Recueil contre l'Extrait du S. N. Avocat du Roy au Chastelet, Paris, 1663, 557 pages plus 65 pages. (The first edition was in 1652.)

Joly, Claude. Traité des Restitutions des Grands, Precedé d'une Lettre touchant quelques points de la Morale Chrestienne, 1665, 96 pages plus 228 pages.

The following is a list of the pamphlets in defense of the opposition which I found significant enough to note:

Accouché (l') espagnole, avec le caquet des politiques, ou le Frère et la suite du Politique Lutin sur les maladies de l'Estat, par le sieur de Sandricourt, Paris, 1652, 23 pages. For Sandricourt see C. Moreau, *Bibliographie des Mazarinades*, I, 7-13.

Advertissement très-important et très-utile au public, touchant le retour du sieur d'Emery, avec l'Arrest de la cour contre Iean Particelly, banqueroutier et faulsaire, et autres complices, du 9 avril, 1620, 1649, 23 pages.

Advis à la Reyne d'Angleterre et à la France, pour servir de réponse à l'Autheur qui en a représenté l'aveuglement, 1650, 7 pages.

Advis à la Reyne, sur la conférence de Ruel, Paris, Robert Sara, 1649, 4 pages.

Advis important et nécessaire, aux Corps de Ville, Bourgeois et Citoyens de la Ville de Paris, sur la prochaine élection d'un Prevost des Marchands, Par lequel, par de grandes et importantes raisons, il leur est monstré que, pour le bien et salut de la Ville, il est nécessaire de procéder à l'élection d'un Prevost des Marchands suivant les anciens Droicts et Usages, et comme il a esté pratiqué dans l'élection de M. de Broussel, Conseiller en Parlement, sans plus recevoir Ordre ny

Lettre de Cachet de la Cour ny d'une autre Puissance, comme contraire aux Ordonnances; avec la Response aux Objections contraires, et les moyens pour se restablir dans cet ancien Droict d'Election, Paris, André Chouqueux, 1652, 24 pages.

Agréable récit de ce qui s'est passé aux dernières barricades de Paris, décrites en vers burlesques, Paris, Nicolas Bessin, 1649, 23 pages.

Anathème (l') et l'excommunication d'un ministre d'Estat estranger, Tiré de l'Escriture Saincte, Paris, Mathieu Colombel, 1649, 12 pages.

Antidote (l') au venin des libelles du *Royaliste à Agathon* et de la *vérité nuë*, Paris, 1652, 32 pages.

Apologie de Messieurs du Parlement, respondant, de poinct en poinct, au Libelle intitulé: Les *Sentiments d'un Fidel Suiet du Roy sur l'Arrest du Parlement, du 29 décembre 1651*, Paris, 1652, 40 pages.

Apologie des Frondeurs, 1650, 11 pages.

Apologie des Normans au Roy pour la iustification de leurs armes, Paris, Cardin Besongne, 1649, 12 pages.

Apologie du Révérend Pére Chartreux contre le Pére Faure sur la Response à la Harangue faite à la Reyne, Paris, 1652, 24 pages.

Apologie pour Messieurs les Princes, envoyée par madame de Longueville à Messieurs du Parlement de Paris, [1650,] 87 pages. Moreau has 37 pages. This is one of the few errors I have found in his work.

L'Asne rouge dépeint avec tous ses déffauts en la personne du Cardinal Mazarin: 1° sur son incapacité et maniement des affaires; 2° sur son ignorance et ambition démesurée; 3° sur ses actions et entreprises qui font cognoistre ses trahisons et perfidies contre l'Estat, Paris, Louis Hardouin, 1652, 20 pages plus 24 pages.

Authoritè (l') des Roys, des Princes, des Républiques et des Parlemens, présenté au Roy, dans la Ville de Pontoise, par un grand Prélat, Paris, 1652, 31 pages.

Aveuglement de la France depuis la minorité, 3 parts of 31, 31 et 32 pages.

Bon (le) ministre d'Estat, Paris, Jacques Guillery, 1649, 12 pages.

Bransle-Mazarin (le), Dansé au souper de quelques-uns de ce party là chez M. Renard, où monsieur de Beaufort donna le bal, Paris, 1649, 6 pages.

Caducée (le) d'Estat, faisant voir par la Raison et par l'Histoire: 1° Que nous ne pouvons point espérer de Paix pendant que la Reyne sera dans le Conseil; 2° Que l'entrée du Conseil est interdite à la Reyne par les Loix de l'Estat; 3° Que la Reyne est obligée de se retirer en son appanage, pour ses seuls interests et pour son honneur; 4° Qu'on ne peut point dire que Mazarin est chassé pendant que la Reyne sera dans le Conseil et que pour cette raison le Roy est obligé de faire retirer la Reyne; 5° Que les tendresses de fils ne doivent point faire aucune impression dans l'esprit du Roy, pour l'obliger à retenir sa Mère dans le Conseil, si sa présence y est contraire au repos de l'Estat; 6° Et que si la Reyne ayme son fils, elle doit consentir à cette retraitte sans aucune résistance, Paris, Pierre Le Muet, 1652, 32 pages. This is by Dubosc Montandré. For this person see C. Moreau, *Bibliographie des Mazarinades*, I, 27-32.

Catalogue des Partisans, ensemble leur généalogie et extraction, vie, moeurs et fortunes, 1649, 20 pages.

Catéchisme (le) de la cour, Paris, Philippe Clément, 1652, 8 pages plus 8 pages.

Catéchisme des partisans ou Résolutions théologiques touchant l'Imposition, Levées et Employ des Finances, dressé par Demandes et Réponses, pour plus grande facilité, par le R. P. D. P. D. S. I., Paris, Cardin Besongne, 1649, 32 pages.

Censeur (le) du temps et du monde, portant en main la clef promise du *Politique lutin*, ou des *Visions d'Alectromante*, etc., de *l'Accouchée Espagnole*, etc., de la *Descente du Politique Lutin aux Limbes*, Des *Préparatifs*, etc., Et de la *France en travail, sans pouvoir accoucher faute de Sage-femme* par le sieur de Sandricourt, Paris, 1652, 55 pages plus 46 pages plus 48 pages plus 71 pages.

Champagne (la) désolée par l'Armée d'Erlach, Paris, 1649, 8 pages.

Complot (le) et entretien burlesque sur l'arrest du 29 décembre, contenant les principaux chefs d'accusation proposez par la France contre le Ministère du Cardinal Mazarin, par le sieur de Sandricourt, Paris, 1652, 23 pages.

Conférence (la) des députez de Son Altesse royale à Saint-Germain-en-Laye sur l'ouverture de la Paix, faite par le Roy d'Angleterre; Sa Harangue à sa Majesté, avec les propositions de Messieurs les députiez et l'impertinente response du Cardinal Mazarin, Paris, Jean Brunet, 1652, 8 pages.

Contract (le) de mariage du Parlement avec la Ville de Paris, Paris, veuve Guillemot, [1649,] 8 pages.

Coq à l'asne ou Lettre burlesque du sieur Voiture ressuscité au preux chevalier Guischens, aliàs le mareschal de Grammont, sur les affaires et nouvelles du temps, Paris chez la veufve et héritiers de l'Autheur, ruë Bon-Conseil, à l'enseigne du bout du Monde, 1649, 8 pages.

Courier (le) bourdelois apportant toutes les nouvelles de Bourdeaux, tant dedans la ville que de hors, Paris, Jean Le Rat, 1649, 7 plus 5 plus 7 pages.

Courrier (le) du temps, apportant ce qui se passe de plus secret en la Cour des Princes de l'Europe, [Amsterdam, Jean Sansonius,] 1649, 32 pages.

Croysade pour la conservation du Roy et du Royaume, Paris, 1652, 7 pages.

Décadence (la) visible de la royauté, reconnuë par cinq marques infaillibles: 1. par le peu d'authorité que ceux qui sont interessez à la soutenir ont auprès de Sa Majesté; 2. par le peu de respect que les peuples ont pour tout ce qui vient de la part du Roy; 3. par l'usage des fourbes que le Conseil fait pratiquer à Sa Majesté, pour abuser de la simplicité des peuples; 4. par la facilité des entreprises ausquelles on porte Sa Majesté, sans les concerter comme il faut pour les faire réüssir à son honneur; 5. et par le secours que le Conseil luy fait emprunter des Huguenots, en les restablissant dans leurs privilèges, pour faire triompher le party Mazarin avec plus de succez, 1652, 16 pages. This is by Dubosc Montandré.

Décision de la question du temps, à la Reyne régente, Paris, Cardin Besongne, 1649, 15 pages.

Descente (la) du polit. lutin aux limbes sur l'Enfance et les Maladies de l'Estat, par le sieur de Sandricourt. Demande au Vendeur le *Politique Lutin* et *l'Accouchée Espagnolle;* car en voici la suitte, Paris, 1652, 24 pages.

Désespoir (le) de Mazarin sur la condamnation de sa mort, et l'adveu qu'il faict de tous ces crimes, en faveur de Messieurs les Princes et des Bourgeois de Paris, présenté à Son Altesse Royale, Paris, 1652, 15 pages.

Dialogue entre le Roy de bronze et la Samaritaine sur les affaires du temps présent, Paris, Arnould Cotinet, 1649, 8 plus 7 plus 8 pages.

Discours au Parlement sur la détention des Princes, [1650,] 31 pages.

Discours chrestien et politique de la puissance des Roys, 32 pages.

Discours sur la députation du Parlement à M. le Prince de Condé, [1649,] 11 pages.

Discussion (la) des quatre controverses politiques. I. Si la Puissance des Roys est de droict Divin, et si elle est absoluë. II. Si les Roys sont par dessus les Loix. III. Si les Peuples ou Estats Generaux ont pouvoir de regler leur Puissance. IV. Si dans l'estat ou se trouve maintenant les affaires, on peut faire un Regent ou Lieutenant pour le Roy, 24 pages.

Donion (le) du droit naturel divin contre toutes les attaques des Ennemis de Dieu et de ses peuples, donnant la Camusade au Très-Illustre Grammairien de Samothrace. "Revelatur ira Dei de Coelo, super omnem impietatem et iniustitiam hominum eorum, qui veritatem Dei in iniustitia detinent." Ad Rom., Cap. I, vers. 18, Paris, 1649, 12 pages.

Écho (l') lugubre de la France, avec l'oppression de la ville de Paris, et les ruses du Renard Sicilien descouvertes, Paris, Jacques Guillery, 1649, 7 pages.

Enfer (l'), le purgatoire et le paradis temporel de la France, Paris, François Preuveray, 1649, 8 pages.

Entretien (l') familier du Roy avec monsieur le duc d'Aniou, son frère, à sainct germain en laye Fidèlement recueilli par un des officiers de Sa Majesté, Paris, Henry Sara, 1649, 8 pages.

Entretien secret de messieurs de la cour de Saint-Germain avec messieurs de la cour de Parlement de Paris, Paris, Jean Hénault, 1649, 23 pages.

Épilogue, ou Dernier appareil du bon citoyen sur les misères publiques, [Paris, Robert Sara,] 1649, 11 pages.

Factum pour Messieurs les Princes, [1650,] 36 pages.

France (la) désolée aux pieds du Roy, où le Gouvernement Tyrannique de Mazarin est succinctement descrit, nulli fas Italo tantam subvertere gentem, Virg. [1649,] 8 pages.

France (la) en travail sans pouvoir accoucher faute de sage-femme, par le sieur de Sandricourt. C'est une branche de mon *Accouchée Espagnole*, et la Cinquième pièce de mes fictions Politiques la 1e. a esté le *Politique Lutin*, ou les *Visions d'Alectromante*, etc. la 2e. *l'Accouchée Espagnole*, avec le *Cacquet des Politiques*, etc. la 3e. la *Descente du Polit. Lutin aux Limbes*, etc. la 4e. Les *Préparatifs de la Descente du C. Mazarin aux Enfers avec les Entretiens des Dieux souterrains*, etc. Pour la Clef que ie t'ay promis, elle est entre les mains du Graveur. Il te burine quelques feüillages, pour te la rendre plus mignone, Paris, 1652, 39 pages.

Franche (la) marguerite faisant voir: 1° que le Roy ne peut point restablir le Mazarin, et que par conséquent, l'armement qui se fait pour ce dessein, est iniuste; 2° que les Loys fondamentales de l'Estat ne permettent point à la Reyne d'estre chef du Conseil de Sa Majesté, et que par conséquent tout ce qui se fait par son advis, ne doit point estre suivy; 3° que le Roy, quelque majeur qu'il soit, doit nantmoins vivre sous la curatelle, quoy que tacite, de Son Altesse Royale et de ses Princes, iusqu'à l'âge prescrit par les loix pour l'émancipation des enfans; 4° et que pendant cette conjoncture d'affaire, Son Altesse Royale, Mrs les Princes et les Parlemens peuvent commander le ban et l'arrière ban, pour terminer bien-tost cette guerre Mazarine, 16 pages. This is by Dubosc Montandré.

Gazettier (le) des-interessé, et le Testament de Iules Mazarin. *Sur l'imprimé à Paris chez Jean Brunet et Claude Morlot*, 1649, 20 pages.

Harangue (la) célèbre faite à la Reyne sur sa régence, Paris, Toussainct Quinet, 1649, 30 pages.

Harangue faite à la Reyne, au Palais-Royal, le 21 décembre 1648, par M. Amelot, premier Président de la Cour des Aydes, pour la révocation du traité des tailles et le soulagement des Officiers et du Peuple, avec un récit abbrégé de ce qui se passa en la Députation de ladite Cour sur ce sujet, Paris, Denys Langlois, 1649, 10 pages.

Heureuse (l') rencontre d'une mine d'or, trouvée en France pour l'enrichissement du Roy et de ses suiets, Paris, Mathurin Hénault, 1649, 8 pages.

Histoire de la prison et de la liberté de Monsieur le Prince, Paris, Augustin Courbé, 1651, 227 pages.

Icon (l') Traduit de Latin en François, ou le Tableau du Tyran Mazarin, Paris, 1649, 20 pages.

Importantes veritez pour les Parlemens. Protecteurs de l'Estat, conservateurs des Loix, et Peres du Peuple. Tirées des anciennes Ordonnances et Loix fondamentales du Royaume. Dediee au Roy. Par I. A. D. *Utcumque ferent hoc fata, Vincit amor patriae laudumque immensa cupido*, Paris, Iaques Villery, 1649, 95 pages.

Iniuste (l') au throsne de la fortune, ou le Fléau de la France, Paris, Nicolas Jacquard, 1649, 11 pages.

Innocence (l') des armes de Monsieur le Prince, Iustifiée par les Loix de la Conscience. Bordeaux, G. de la Court, 1651, 28 pages.

Inventaire des merveilles du monde rencontrées dans le palais du cardinal Mazarin, Paris, Rolin de La Haye, 1649, 7 pages.

Italie (l') vengée de son tyran par les armes des bons François, par le sieur N. R. (Rosard), champenois, Paris, François Musnier, 1649, 8 pages.

Iuliade (la), ou Iules démasqué, Où se voit au vif le caractère de son âme, par le sieur De La Campie, gentilhomme Périgordin, Paris, veufve François Targa, 1649, 12 pages.

Iustification (la) du Parlement et de la ville de Paris dans la prise des armes contre l'oppression et Tyrannie du Cardinal Mazarin, Paris, Alexandre Lesselin, 1649, 19 pages.

Lettre à monsieur le cardinal, burlesque, Paris, Arnould Cotinet, 1649, 20 pages.

Lettre d'avis à messieurs du Parlement de Paris, escrite par un provincial, Paris, 1649, 34 pages.

Lettre d'un gentil-homme à la Reyne, Paris, veuve Théod. Pépingué et Est. Maucroy, 1649, 8 pages.

Lettre d'un gentil-homme désintéressé à messieurs les députez des Estats, sur les mouvemens presens, et des moyens qu'ils doivent tenir pour les pacifier, Paris, 1652, 15 pages.

Lettre d'un marguiller de Paris à son curé sur la conduite de Monseigneur le coadiuteur, Paris, 1651, 19 pages.

Lettre d'un religieux envoyée à monseigneur le prince de Condé, à Saint-Germain-en-Laye, contenant la verité de la vie et moeurs du Cardinal Mazarin, avec exhortation audit Seigneur Prince d'abandonner son party, Paris, Rolin de La Haye, 1649, 11 pages.

Lettre d'une religieuse présentée au Roy et à la reine régente, le premier février 1649, pour obtenir la paix, Paris, Guillaume Sassier, 1649, 7 pages.

Lettre de monsieur le duc d'Espernon à un de messieurs du Parlement de Paris, avec la Response, 1650, 35 pages.

Lettre de monsieur le mareschal de Ranzau, gouverneur de Dunquerque, à monseigneur le duc d'Orleans, Paris, Rolin de La Haye, 1649, 8 pages.

Lettre de Pierre de Provence à la Reyne, En forme d'avis, sur ce qui s'est passé en son Pays, Paris, Jean Hénault, 1649, 11 pages.

Lettre du cardinal Antonio Barberin, envoyée de Rome au cardinal Mazarin à Sainct-Germain-en-Laye, Touchant les troubles de France, Paris, vefue André Musnier, 1649, 8 pages.

Lettre du Cardinal Mazarin escrite au comte Pigneranda, Plénipotentiaire d'Espagne pour la paix générale à Munster, par laquelle se iustifie le mauvais dessein du Cardinal Mazarin, tant sur la ville de Paris que sur tout l'Estat, Paris, François Noël, 1649, 7 pages.

Lettre du chevalier Georges de Paris à monseigneur le prince de Condé, Paris, [Nicolas Boisset], 1649, 18 pages.

Lettre du Parlement de Metz à monseigneur le duc d'Orléans, Lieutenant Général du Royaume pendant l'absence et la captivité du Roy, touchant la retraite du cardinal Mazarin dedans la ville et citadelle de Metz, Paris, Jacob Chevalier, 1652, 7 pages.

Lettre du père Michel, religieux hermite de l'ordre des Camaldoli près Grosbois, à monseigneur le duc d'Engoulesme sur les cruautez des mazarinistes en Brie, Paris, 1649, 32 pages.

Lettre du sieur de Nacar à l'abbé de La Rivière, à Saint-Germain-en-Laye, le 9 février 1649, contenant le grand nombre des pièces imprimées contre Jules Mazarin, Paris, Jean Brunet, 1649, 10 pages.

Lettre (la) du sieur Pepoly, comte bolognois, escrite au cardinal Mazarin, pour sa retraite hors de la France, 1649, 8 pages.

Lettre déchiffrée d'un mazariniste à Mazarin, trouvée entre Saint-Germain et Paris, et traduite d'Italien en François, sur le Mariage du Parlement avec la Ville de Paris, Paris, Arnould Cotinet, 1649, 7 pages.

Lettre envoyée sur le suiet de l'assemblée de la noblesse, et des procurations escrites dans les provinces, Paris, veuve I. Guillemot, 1651, 8 pages.

Lettre escrite au chevalier de La Valette, Sous Le Nom du Peuple de Paris, avec la response aux placards qu'il a semez par ladite Ville, Paris, 1649, 8 pages.

Lettre escrite de Madrid par un gentilhomme espagnol à un sien amy, par laquelle il luy descouvre une partie des intrigues du Cardinal Mazarin, traduitte de l'Espagnol en François, Paris, veuve J. Guillemot, 1649, 7 pages.

Lettre politique sur l'Assemblée de la Noblesse, [1651,] 7 pages.

Lettres de deux amis Sur la prise de la Bastille, 1649, 8 pages.

Lunettes (les) à toutes âges, pour faire voir clair aux Ennemis de l'Estat, Paris, vefve Iean Remy, 1649, 8 pages.

Manifeste de madame la duchesse de Longueville, Bruxelles, Iean Roxh, 1650, 12 pages.

Manifeste (le) de Mademoiselle, présenté aux coeurs généreux par le sieur C. Perret, Paris, 1652, 16 pages.

Manuel du bon citoyen, ou Bouclier de défense légitime Contre les assauts de l'Ennemy, 1649, 24 pages.

Maximes morales et chrestiennes pour le repos des consciences dans les affaires présentes, Pour servir d'instruction aux Curez, et aux Confesseurs, aux Prédicateurs, dressées et envoyées de Saint-Germain-en-Laye par un Théologien, fidèle Officier du Roy, à messieurs du Parlement, Paris, Cardin Besongne, 1649, 16 pages plus 30 pages.

Mot (le) à l'oreille, ou le Miroir qui ne flatte point, Paris, 1649, 7 pages.

Moyens infaillibles pour faire périr le Cardinal Mazarin, et la guerre à ses despens, Paris, vefve I. Guillemot, 1652, 6 pages.

Observations veritables et dés-intéressées sur un escrit imprimé au Louvre, intitulé: *les Sentiments d'un fidelle suiet du Roy Contre l'arrest du Parlement du 29 Décembre*, 1651 Par lesquelles l'authorité du Parlement et la Iustice de son Arrest contre le Mazarin est plainement déffenduë, et l'imposteur qui le condamne, entièrement refuté, Par un bon Ecclésiastique très fidelle sujet du Roy, première partie. *Qui justificat impium, et qui condemnat iustum, abominabilis est uterque apud Deum.* Prov., cap. 17, vers. 15, Paris, 1652, 152 pages.

Ombre (l') du grand Armand, cardinal, duc de Richelieu, parlante à Iules Mazarin, Paris, [François Noël,] 1649, 11 pages.

Passe-port (le), et l'adieu de Mazarin, en vers burlesques, Paris, Claude Huot, 1649, 11 pages.

Pierre (la) de touche aux Mazarins, Paris, 1652, 40 pages.

Plainte du Carnaval et de la foire Saint-Germain, en vers burlesques, Paris, Claude Huot, 1649, 8 pages.

Plaintes et réflexions politiques sur la harangue de M. l'Archevesque de Roüen faite au Roy dedans la ville de Tours, au nom du clergé de France et de vingt-quatre Evesques suivans la Cour qui l'accompagnoient, contre le Parlement de Paris, en faveur du cardinal Mazarin proscript et légitimement condamné par plusieurs Arrests donnez contre luy, où il est monstré que le Parlement est Juge naturel et légitime des

Cardinaux, Archevesques, Evesques Abbes et autres Ecclesiastiques du Royaume, tant Séculiers que Réguliers, 1652, 22 pages.

Politique (le) burlesque, dédié à Amaranthe, par S. T. F. S. L. S. D. T., Paris, 1649, 44 pages.

Politique (le) lutin porteur des ordonnances, ou les Visions d'Alectromante sur les maladies de l'Estat, par le sieur de Sandricourt, Paris, 1652, 24 pages.

Préparatifs (les) de la descente du cardinal Mazarin aux enfers, avec les Entretiens des Dieux sousterrains, Touchant et Contre les *Maximes* supposées *véritables du gouvernement de la France* iustifié par l'ordre des temps dans toutes les Races Royales, par le sieur de Sandricourt. C'est la suite de ma *Descente aux limbes.* Tu demanderas au Vendeur les trois pièces précédentes, Paris, 1652, 32 pages.

Question canonique, si Monsieur le Prince a peu prendre les Armes en conscience, et si ceux qui prennent son party offensent Dieu. Contre les theologiens Courtisans, Bordeaux, G. de la Court, 1651, 23 pages.

Question: S'il y doit avoir un premier ministre dans le conseil du Roy; raison d'Estat et politique très-importante à décider pour le bien du Souverain et pour le Repos de la Patrie, Paris, 1649, 22 pages.

Questions, en forme de dialogue, du Conseil de Conscience, au Conseil d'Estat, avec les Responses, Paris, François Noël, 1649, 7 pages.

Raisonnable (le) plaintif sur la dernière déclaration du Roy, Paris, Jacques Bellé, 1652, 14 pages.

Raisons d'Estat contre le ministère estranger, [1649,] 7 pages.

Raisons (les) ou les Motifs véritables de la déffense du Parlement et des Habitans de Paris contre les Perturbateurs du repos public et les Ennemis du Roy et de l'Estat, Paris, 1649, 26 pages.

Récit véritable de tout ce qui s'est fait et passé en l'Assemblée générale de la Noblesse tenuë à la Roche-Guyon, avec la Lettre de Cachet du Roy envoyée à ladite Assemblée, Paris, veufve Guillemot, 1652, 7 pages.

Remonstrance officieuse des Bordelois aux Parisiens de tous les ordres contre le retour du Cardinal Mazarin. Sur un imprimé à Bordeaux, Paris, Iacob Chevalier, 1652, 16 pages.

Réplique au suffisant et captieux Censeur de la *Lettre d'Avis présentée au Parlement par un Provincial,* [1649,] 7 pages.

Requeste burlesque des partisans au Parlement, Paris, Jacques Guillery, 1649, 8 pages.

Requeste de la Noblesse pour l'assamblée des Estats généraux, Paris, veufve Guillemot, 1651, 15 pages.

Requeste des trois Estats, présentée à messieurs du Parlement, 1648, 8 pages.

Requeste (la) des trois Estats Touchant le lieu et les Personnes qu'on doit choisir pour l'Assemblée des Estats Généraux, Conformé à la proposition que Son Altesse Royale en a fait à Leurs Maiestez, Et aux sentimens de Messieurs les Princes, dont les Conseils doivent estre principalement suivis et preferez à tous autres, [1651,] 24 pages.

Requête des peuples de France, affligés des présents troubles, à nos seigneurs de la cour de Parlement, séant à Paris, 1652, 20 pages.

Response de Messieurs les Princes aux calomnies et impostures du Mazarin, 1650, 50 pages.

Response de monseigneur le Prince, et ses très-humbles Remonstrances faites au Roy, à la Reine Regente, et à la France. Sur le suiet de sa Detention, 1651, 91 pages.

Response des bourgeois d'Orléans faite à Sa Maiesté et la députation qu'ils ont envoyée à Son Altesse Royale, touchant le dessein qu'ils ont de ne permettre point l'entrée de Mazarin dans leur ville, 1652, 8 pages.

Résultat de l'assemblée de la noblesse tenue à Dreux par les Députez des Baillages unis, le Dimanche vingt-uniesme Iuillet mil six cens cinquante-deux, Ensemble le Récit par le menu de ce que leurs Deputez en Cour y ont négocié, et de toute leur conduite, Paris, veufve I. Guillemot, 1652, 8 pages.

Royal (le) au Mazarin, Luy faisant voir par la raison et par l'histoire, 1. que l'authorité des Roys sur la vie et sur le bien des subjets est fort limitée, à moins qu'elle ne soit tirannique; 2. que l'authorité des Princes du Sang est essentielle dans le gouvernement; 3. que l'authorité des autres Parlements de France pour les affaires d'Estat est inférieure et subordonnée à celle du Parlement de Paris; 4. que les Prélats n'ont point d'authorité dans le maniement des affaires d'Estat, et que leur devoir les engage à n'avoir d'attachement que pour le sanctuaire, [1652,] 32 pages. This is by Dubosc Montandré.

Second Discours d'Estat et de Religion, a messieurs du Parlement, Paris, Nicolas Iacquard, 1648, 12 pages.

Seconde (la) lettre du chevalier Georges à monsieur le prince, Paris, I. Brunet, 1649, 8 pages.

Sommaire de la doctrine curieuse du cardinal Mazarin, par luy déclarée en une lettre qu'il escrit à un sien Confident, pour se purger de l'Arrest du Parlement et des Faicts dont il est accusé. Ensemble la response à icelle, par laquelle il est dissuadé de se représenter au Parlement, Paris, Nicolas Bessin, 1649, 18 pages.

Tableau (le) du tyran Mazarin, 20 pages.

Tarif du prix dont on est convenu dans une assemblée de Notables, tenue en présence de Messieurs les Princes, pour récompenser ceux qui délivreront la France du Mazarin, qui a esté iustement condamné par Arrest du Parlement, Paris, Nicolas Vivenay, 1652, 15 pages.

Théologien (le) d'État à la reyne, Paris, Jean du Bray, 1649, 12 pages plus 20 pages.

Théologien (le) politique, Pièce curieuse sur les affaires du Temps pour la défense des bons François, Paris, Guillaume et Jean-Baptiste Loyson, 1649, 11 pages.

Theses d'Estat, tirees de la Politique Chrestienne Presentees a monseigneur le Prince de Conty, Paris, veufve Theod. Pepingue' et Est. Maucroy, 1649, 12 pages.

Union (l'), ou Association des Princes sur l'iniuste Détention du Prince de Condé, Conty, et Duc de Longueville, *Iouxte la Copie imprimée à Bourdeaux*, 1650, 11 pages.

Véritables (les) maximes du gouvernement de la France Iustifiées par l'ordre des temps, depuis l'establissement de la Monarchie iusques à présent, Servant de Response au prétendu Arrest de cassation du Conseil, du 18 Ianvier 1652. Dédié à Son Altesse Royale, Paris, veufve I. Guillemot, 1652, 23 pages plus 15 pages.

Vérité (la) prononçant ses oracles sans flatterie: 1. sur la Reyne; 2. sur le Roy; 3. sur le Duc d'Orléans; 4. sur le prince de Condé; 5. sur le Parlement; 6. sur le Duc de Beaufort; 7. sur le Coadjuteur; 8. sur le Parlement de Pontoise; 9. sur Paris et sur l'Estat, 1652, 40 pages plus 39 pages.

Vérité (la) toute nue, ou Advis sincère et des-interessé sur les véritables causes des maux de l'Estat, et les moyens d'y apporter le remède, Paris, 1652, 23 pages.

Vray amateur de la paix contre les advis dangereux du Libelle intitule: *Advis salutaires et généreux*, etc., Paris, Nicolas de La Vigne, 1649, 22 pages.

Vray (le) courtisan sans flaterie, Qui déclare ce que c'est que l'Authorité Royale, Paris, Veufve d'Antoine Coulon, 1649, 16 pages.